WEE GLESCA
A POCKET GUIDE TO GLASGOW
SCOTT C DOCHERTY

Wee Glesca

My Pocket Guide to Glasgow

By

Scott C. Docherty
Top-Ten-Glasgow-Guide.com

Early 2015 Edition

Dedicated to the memory of those who lost their
lives in the **Clutha Bar** & **Queen Street** tragedies
and to their loved ones and the people of Glasgow
who rallied around them

wee glesca

welcome & thanks

Welcome to Wee Glesca, the pocket guide to Glasgow created by me, Scott Docherty, owner of the Top Ten Glasgow Guide. Thank you so much for picking up a copy, and I really hope you enjoy it!

Since the first edition was published in 2014, thanks to folks like you my little guide became the number one best selling Glasgow travel guide on Amazon, and it was just breathtaking hearing some of the kind feedback I received. Seeing my very own book pop out of that familiar cardboard Amazon envelope for the first time made me beam with pride, but it was the reaction from those who'd spent their hard-earned money to trust me enough to buy or download it that *really* made me tingle with excitement (*alright, steady on Docherty!*)

It's all inspired me to make sure this new edition is packed to the brim with even more up to date insider information on my home town, so I really hope you enjoy and get great use of this improved version of the book. I'd love to hear from you about how you've used it, and what you enjoyed most about visiting or living in the City, so please make sure to leave a wee comment on Amazon or send me some feedback directly on the contact form on my site. You can also reach me on Twitter (@toptenglasgow), Facebook (/toptenglasgowguide) & Pinterest (/toptenglasgow).

what's *not* in it?

There's a few reasons why this guide, written by someone who doesn't work for the tourist industry (that's me!), differs from the others you'll come across. Unlike most glossy travel guides on the City, in Wee Glesca you will *not* find:

- A lengthy history of the City you could find online in a heartbeat if you were really interested;
- Pointless climate details and weather trends. When it boils down to it, you get here, you look out the window, you dress appropriately. Enough said!
- Fancy pictures taken by professionals, designed to make the place look fantastic (which it really is), but which just increase the size of the book when all you really need is the right information;
- Travel writer verbal diarrhoea, with flowery language most Glaswegians would just find totally ridiculous;
- Cool looking maps you can't follow. Future editions may include a map or two, but for the most part you would be better served getting a guide like this and a proper fold-up map;
- Endless lists of hotels. Let's be honest, before you travel here you'll likely find a place to stay, so why would you want your guidebook you take with you stuffed with hotels, telling you where else you could've stayed?

what *is* in it?

Well, pretty much all you need to squeeze the most out of your visit here. Top ten lists of:

- Arts & history attractions, shopping hotspots, music venues, theatres, restaurants, festivals, new hidden gems and more;
- Telephone numbers, addresses, opening times, & links to websites, Twitter feeds and Facebook pages;
- Bang up to date information. Most guides are fairly out of date, this one isn't!
- Information from me, a real insider, a local, a dude who lives here and sees with his own eyes how best to experience Glasgow day in day out;
- Everything nicely drilled down and packaged so you can bookmark what you need.

legal stuff

how to use this guide
You've done the hard part by buying it. Now, feel free to treat it how you want. Stuff it in your bag (yes, I'm still getting stick because it can't actually fit in your pocket!), highlight bits, write on the spaces I've left under each part, blow your nose with it...

You'll see that I've broken everything into handy sections of top 10s in no particular order, all indexed in the contents page. Each item has a description, contact details & website and social media addresses.

So I hope using Wee Glesca makes visiting my home town just a wee bit easier.

Yours aye,
Scott

contents

SO HERE'S THE THING...

Keep up with <u>what's on in Glasgow every weekend</u> with my regular list. I publish it every week unless I don't get the chance. And you can sign up for my free email list while you're there if you want first dibs on what's going on.

> top-ten-glasgow-guide.com/whats-on-in-glasgow-this-weekend.html

OH, AND ANOTHER THING...

If you're organising an event in Glasgow and want to spread the word in advance, why not <u>have it featured on my site</u>? I'll give you a dedicated page for a month, and will make some noise on Twitter, Facebook & Google+ for you.

> top-ten-glasgow-guide.com/whats-on-glasgow-events.html

getting around

top-ten-glasgow-guide.com
facebook.com/toptenglasgowguide
twitter.com/toptenglasgow

WEE GLESCA
A POCKET GUIDE TO GLASGOW

the clockwork orange (glasgow subway)

lowdown

The Glasgow subway is by far the easiest way to navigate the centre, east and west of the City.

It's the world's 3rd oldest underground system and is called by the locals "the clockwork orange" in recognition of the historical colour of the old subway trains.

It's entirely underground, runs in a circle clockwise & anti-clockwise and takes only 24 minutes to go round the 15 stations, running about every 4 minutes at peak times, so if you miss one it won't be long until the next!

It costs as little as £1.40 for a single trip, £2.70 for an all day travel pass, and £13 for a 7 day pass. Kids get in for half price. There are plenty of other ticket options including park & ride and travel cards as well.

Oh, and search for "Glasgow subcrawl" for a bit of fun while you're here – drink at every station & see where you end up!

contact
Tel: +44 141 332 6811
Email: enquiry@spt.co.uk

social
spt.co.uk/subway
facebook.com/glasgowsubway
twitter.com/glasgowsubway

when
6.30am-11.45pm Mon-Sat
10am-6.12pm Sun

where
Check website for stations

top-ten-glasgow-guide.com
facebook.com/toptenglasgowguide
twitter.com/toptenglasgow

WEE GLESCA
A POCKET GUIDE TO GLASGOW

jump a taxi

lowdown

All taxis here must be fully licensed, and the way to tell this is by looking for the licence displayed inside and outside of the taxi before you get in. Don't trust any without a licence! There are three types of taxi in Glasgow you need to know.

Mainly you'll see black hackney taxis milling around town, or the same type covered in adverts. They're run by Glasgow Taxis, and can be flagged down whenever you see one without its orange light switched on, unless you're close to the taxi rank. If you're travelling far remember to ask if the driver will apply a boundary charge, & if possible try and agree a fare in advance.

There are private operators running more usual types of vehicle but they all have their details displayed. They're generally cheaper, but can't be flagged down & you have to call them in advance. Best to use these if you're heading out of the centre.

There's also the airport taxis, most of which are white, and again have to be called in advance.

Remember to tip your driver for a good journey by at least rounding the fare up to the nearest few pounds.

contact

Glasgow Taxis: +44 141 429 7070
Hampden Cabs (south): +44 141 332 5050
Eastwood Mearns (south): +44 141 644 5353
Glasgow Private Hire (east): +44 141 774 3000
Great Western Taxis (west): +44 141 942 7777
Glasgow Airport Taxis: +44 141 889 1813 (phone in advance for discount)

note

Some of the private taxi companies give a bigger discount if you book online or download their app, so search the companies here. Also, ask your hotel receptionist / restaurant manager etc. to recommend local companies.

3

top-ten-glasgow-guide.com
facebook.com/toptenglasgowguide
twitter.com/toptenglasgow

WEE GLESCA
A POCKET GUIDE TO GLASGOW

train guide

lowdown

Our trains here are operated by Scotrail, with First Group (who operate most of our buses) running it until 1st April 2015 when Abellio takes over.

Whoever runs it though you can rest assured that our train system is highly efficient. Of course every system has its faults and delays from time to time, but by and large I've never had any major difficulties jumping the train here.

The information and services are accessible and easy to follow, so all you need to do to plan your journey is to visit the website, enter your travel plans and you'll be pointed in the right direction. The website has up to date details on routes, ticket prices, delays and offers, so is always the best place to start planning.

Our main stations in the centre of town are Glasgow Central for trains west & south of the City (including to England & Wales), and Glasgow Queen Street for trains east & north.

contact
Tel: 0330 303 0112
Email:
scotrailcustomer.relations@firstgroup.com

social
scotrail.co.uk/
facebook.com/ScotRail
twitter.com/scotrail

when
Check website for all info, train routes, times & stations.

where
Check website for all info, train routes, times & stations.

top-ten-glasgow-guide.com
facebook.com/toptenglasgowguide
twitter.com/toptenglasgow

WEE GLESCA
A POCKET GUIDE TO GLASGOW

catching the right bus

lowdown

As with our trains here, the bus service you'll get from First Bus is regular and efficient around Glasgow, albeit with the odd exception as with every travel service.

Best thing to do using the bus in the City when you're not too familiar with your way around, is to use the First website in advance to plan your journey, get the ticket price (as you won't get change on the bus), and see if there are any deals or offers applicable.

If you get on the bus and aren't sure when to get off, feel free to ask a friendly face or the driver and I'm sure you'll get the right advice.

If you're using the bus to get to and from Glasgow, if First don't work the route then try Stagecoach and National Express, as they're the most frequent in and out of the City, running mainly through Buchanan Street Station opposite the Royal Concert Hall.

And if you're needing a private coach hire to get a larger number of you around when you get here, I'd recommend Croft Mini Coaches first, and the link to their site is below.

contact

Tel: +44 141 420 7600 (First)
Email: Use contact form on websites

social

firstgroup.com/ukbus/glasgow/
twitter.com/FirstinGlasgow
stagecoachbus.com/
nationalexpress.com/home.aspx
croftminicoaches.co.uk/

when

Check websites for all info, bus routes, times & stops.

where

Check websites for all info, bus routes, times & stops.

5

top-ten-glasgow-guide.com
facebook.com/toptenglasgowguide
twitter.com/toptenglasgow

WEE GLESCA
A POCKET GUIDE TO GLASGOW

walking tours

lowdown

Not only does Glasgow house over 70 parks, widespread woodland & inner-city heritage treks, and more trees that you could shake a branch at, it also has a deep and successful commitment to preserving the ecology & wildlife all throughout the City, despite the potentially damaging urban regeneration constantly biting at its ankles.

It stands magnificently with the Clyde Valley as without doubt *the* most important gateway to Scotland & our world famous Munros and Highlands. And more significantly, after generations of plain ignorance Glasgow finally woke up some time ago to the importance of encouraging her citizens & visitors to look after their health.

So it all boils down to the fact that if you prefer walking, when you visit and set out on one of the unique walks Glasgow lays out for you, well, you're in for a treat!

Heading out on one of the superb walking tours, or even just rambling about, will unlock for you a treasure vault of history, heritage & culture you'd simply miss out on if you weren't on foot, and the crackerjack fact about walking in Glasgow is that it's a pretty small city, in which everything you'll want to see is just a wee trek away.

The best walks Glasgow has dotted around the place can be completed in the City Centre, or can be started in Glasgow and finished elsewhere. Here are a few to consider as you put your boots on:

social

top-ten-glasgow-guide.com/walks-glasgow.html
gsa.ac.uk/visit-gsa/city-walking-tours/
greetinglasgow.com/
west-highland-way.co.uk/
walkhighlands.co.uk/glasgow/clyde-walkway.shtml

6

top-ten-glasgow-guide.com
facebook.com/toptenglasgowguide
twitter.com/toptenglasgow

WEE GLESCA
A POCKET GUIDE TO GLASGOW

car hire guide

lowdown

I've hired cars in foreign countries & unfamiliar territories before, and for me the most important thing to investigate isn't the cost and how many suitcases you can fit in the boot, it's the rules of the road applicable where I'll be driving.

Here you need to look at the Highway Code. Main speed limits are 30mph in urban areas, 70mph on motorways. You can't use your mobile phone (cell) while driving. You drive on the left, give way to the right, and stop at *every* red light. The drink driving limits have been reduced to the extent now that if you have a pint of beer or glass of wine, you'll be over the limit and will be prosecuted if stopped by police.

Aside from that, just use common sense. Save oodles by using an online broker in advance to hire the car rather than waiting until you land at the airport. Print off & inspect your documentation, plan your journey in advance, and inspect & get to know your car before you drive off. If you relax, keep it slow and always assume some reckless driver's about to slam into you, I'm sure you'll be fine!

It's really all about the planning, and please let me know if you'd like any more information about hiring or driving a car here before you travel.

social

top-ten-glasgow-guide.com/car-hire-glasgow-airport.html
gov.uk/browse/driving/highway-code
gov.uk/driving-nongb-licence
expedia.co.uk/car-hire
travelocity.com/Cars

7

top-ten-glasgow-guide.com
facebook.com/toptenglasgowguide
twitter.com/toptenglasgow

WEE GLESGA
A POCKET GUIDE TO GLASGOW

cycling around glasgow

lowdown

Slowly but surely, my happy but heavy old friend Glasgow has woken up to the benefits of the bike. When you look around these days, you'll see folks here and there just ignoring other folks on bicycles, where before you would've seen them look with sheer confusion at these funny little characters on two wheels, lightly weaving their way in and around the traffic congestion with an air of satisfaction, heading out of the city smog and down country paths too narrow for 4x4s.

Because cycling in Glasgow has become normal.

Just another way to get around. People will jump on their bike to commute to work or university, or will mountain bike their way over any obstacle and dirt track they can find here. They'll fill their family with porridge on a Sunday morning then whip them out for a ride around the park. And you'll catch riders whispering past you in the City's growing network of cycle lanes as you absently lick the car window wondering how nice it'd be to get some breeze on your face.

Given the Council's perpetual drive to improve our health, ridding the City of her doctor's note reputation, you'll find cycling in Glasgow is getting easier. Whilst the Glasgow Cycle Network is not yet fully completed, meaning that you'll often ride on a cycle lane which suddenly stops and leaves you to fend with the traffic as usual, as long as you're aware of the Highway Code you should be fine.

And when you head off the main traffic routes and into one of the many cycle-friendly parks or even onto the longer trails out into the looming wonder of Scotland, at your own pace you'll be invigorated like never before by our majestic scenery, wildlife and heritage. Here are some links to get you started:

social

top-ten-glasgow-guide.com/cycling-glasgow.html
glasgow.gov.uk/cycling
pedalforscotland.org/
cycle-route.com/routes/Glasgow-Routes-15.html
thebikestation.org.uk/
mapmyride.com/gb/glasgow-sct/
gov.uk/browse/driving/highway-code

top-ten-glasgow-guide.com
facebook.com/toptenglasgowguide
twitter.com/toptenglasgow

WEE GLESCA

A POCKET GUIDE TO GLASGOW

limo hire

lowdown

There is plenty of choice here when it comes to hiring a limo. Girls young or drunken tend to prefer the pink limo, or more often these days the fire engine limo where they can all wear fireman hats & ogle the driver, and the guys just head straight for the hummer with their chests puffed out in macho pride! If you're planning a wedding, there are plenty of companies with a stock of sedan stretch white or executive black limos for hire, and they're usually the standard choice for prom nights here as well.

It's not just about choosing the most appropriate limousine that matters though. Once you've decided which kind you want, have a look online & in the local phone book for the various local limo hire companies specialising in that type, and instead of jumping in and booking the first package that catches your eye, don't be afraid to ask each company the following questions:

1. Do you have any mid-week, group or other discount for cheap limo hire?

2. Can we decorate the limo or have the chauffeur dress up?
3. When will payment be required?
4. Will you send us written confirmation of the hire details?
5. Are there any cancellation fees?
6. How flexible are the pick-up and drop-off locations?
7. How do we pay for & arrange the limo bar drinks, snacks & music?
8. How many people can we fit into the limousine?
9. Can we arrange a certain route for the chauffeur to take us?
10. Why is your service better than everyone else's?

The answers you get to those questions will help you decide which company suits your own needs the most. The rest really is up to your own imagination!

social

clydevalleylimos.co.uk/
glasgowlimousine.co.uk
glasgow-wedding-cars.co.uk/
allstarlimos.net/
pinklimoco.com/
flaminghotlimos.co.uk/hen-night-limo.htm
echummers.co.uk/

9

top-ten-glasgow-guide.com
facebook.com/toptenglasgowguide
twitter.com/toptenglasgow

WEE GLESCA
A POCKET GUIDE TO GLASGOW

personalised tours

lowdown

A bespoke tour of Glasgow and beyond, tailored for you, catering to your own needs, timescales & requests every step of the way.

The type of people who normally book personalised tours usually want different things out of their time in Glasgow and Scotland. Not one of them has ever been the same. However, what they do have in common is that they're usually more discerning, more demanding, more individual, slightly more adventurous, and without exception, they totally dislike the idea of larger bus tour groups which offer very structured and rigid schedules.

Personalised tours are aimed at those who want to do what they want to do, go where they want to go, and see what they want to see. And if you're not sure of the specifics of a trip, your guide will work with you and discuss exactly what you're

looking for - whether you've got an idea, a particular theme or even just a dream, they tend to make it happen for you. Try the links below & arrange a tour of the City, whisky distilleries, Scotland beyond, historic sites and more, but let me know if you don't find what you'd like.

I've said elsewhere that with this City, sitting ashen-faced on the Glasgow tour bus will ensure that my home town will leave you with nothing more than empty photos for a soon-to-be-dusty album. If you muck right in though, give her something of yourself, only then will Glasgow show you her true colours, and the same applies for everywhere else in Scotland as far as I'm concerned.

social

catswhiskerstours.co.uk/
mini-tours.com/
goscotlandtours.com/featured-glasgow-tours.asp
rabbies.com/

10

top-ten-glasgow-guide.com
facebook.com/toptenglasgowguide
twitter.com/toptenglasgow

WEE GLESGA
A POCKET GUIDE TO GLASGOW

sightseeing bus

lowdown

The reliable hop on, hop off, open top Glasgow tour bus is known affectionately here as the Heidless Bus (in other words, the bus with no head!), and while the best way to see this City is to get right into the thick of it, any time my wife & I go to somewhere new on holiday, we tend to get the tour bus around first, at least to make sure we can get our bearings, to help us firm up on what we plan on visiting. Even more than that though, given the cost of public transport in various places, the fact that you can usually hop on and hop off these kind of sightseeing bus tours, and also that normally your tickets for the tour will last you 48 hours, we've occasionally used the tour bus to get around the place we've been visiting just to save some pennies.

On the Glasgow sightseeing tours, your ticket will last you two consecutive days and will entitle you to 10% off various paid attractions around the place that will be listed on the wee brochure you get with your ticket.

You can also book tickets for the spooky Ghoulish Tour, for the Mackintosh Experience Bus Tour which takes you around the attractions designed by one of our favourite sons, Charles Rennie Mackintosh, and there's also a Kids' Club for the wee lads & lassies. I'm pretty sure they also do a bus tour for the Doors Open days every September, where the paid attractions open their doors for free, so that's well worth booking up for as well.

So whatever you use your Glasgow sightseeing tours ticket for I'm sure you'll enjoy the experience & start working out from the tour where you'll want to spend the rest of your time here.

contact

Tel: +44 141 204 0444
Email:
info@citysightseeingglasgow.co.uk

social

citysightseeingglasgow.co.uk/
facebook.com/citysightseeinggla
sgow
twitter.com/glasgowtour

when

Check the website but usually from 9.30am-4pm every hour Mon-Fri & every half hour at the weekend.

where

153 Queen Street
Glasgow, G1 3BJ
(but hop on & off per your map)

---

top-ten-glasgow-guide.com
facebook.com/toptenglasgowguide
twitter.com/toptenglasgow

WEE GLESGA
A POCKET GUIDE TO GLASGOW

arts & history

kelvingrove art gallery & museum

lowdown

One of THE most visited attractions in the country, the Kelvingrove hosts our largest civic collection, with 22 state-of-the-art galleries & over 8,000 spectacular items of natural history, arms & armour, art and much more.

I can't get enough of this place. Its Spanish Baroque architecture is stunning, the massive halls breathtaking, but if you see anything here I'd make sure you catch the looming LA198 Spitfire, Sir Rodger the Asian Elephant, the Sarcophagus of PaBaSa, Dali's Christ of St. John on the Cross, and Van Gogh's portrait of Alexander Reid.

There's just so much to see and do (particularly for kids, interactive workshops, study & discovery centres abound!), that you really need to set aside at least a few hours and visit for yourself. You might even be lucky to hear the resounding acoustics of the massive Grade One organ which plays regularly throughout the day.

contact

Tel: +44 141 276 9500
Email:
museums@glasgowlife.org.uk

social

glasgowlife.org.uk
facebook.com/kelvingrove.glasgowmuseums
twitter.com/kelvingroveart

when

10am-5pm Mon-Thu
11am-5pm Fri & Sun

where

Argyle Street
Glasgow
G83 8AG

top-ten-glasgow-guide.com
facebook.com/toptenglasgowguide
twitter.com/toptenglasgow

WEE GLESGA
A POCKET GUIDE TO GLASGOW

gallery of modern art (goma)

lowdown

GoMA lives in the house of a slave-loving tobacco lord from the 18th century, but don't let that put you off!

It might be more famous for the iconic image outside of Marochetti's statue of the Duke of Wellington, adorned proudly by students with a traffic cone on his head, but GoMA is *so* much more than that.

It's Scotland's most visited modern art gallery, is entirely free, and hosts a rotation of some of the world's most sought after, thought-provoking exhibitions.

I like to pop in whenever I'm nearby, as the exhibitions, workshops, performances and extensive library of art history & design evolve continuously, so there's always something new to see, particularly during the outstanding Glasgow International Festival of Visual Art every year.

And don't worry about the throng of goths & emos usually hanging around outside, with their sub-cultural darkness & skateboarding antics – they're harmless, and in my mind the fact they find comfort here just reflects how contemporary & unique the place is.

contact

Tel: +44 141 287 3050
Email:
museums@glasgowlife.org.uk

social

glasgowlife.org.uk
facebook.com/galleryofmodernart.glasgowmuseums
twitter.com/glasgowgoma

when

10am-5pm Mon-Wed & Sat
10am-8pm Thu
11am-5pm Fri & Sun

where

Royal Exchange Square
Glasgow
G1 3AH

14

top-ten-glasgow-guide.com
facebook.com/toptenglasgowguide
twitter.com/toptenglasgow

WEE GLESGA

A POCKET GUIDE TO GLASGOW

riverside museum & tall ship

lowdown

There's not many cities who can boast as much as Glasgow a heritage and track record of innovation in world transport & technology. The Riverside Museum of Transport and Travel captures this in great detail, housing within its awe-inspiring architecture over 3,000 exhibits that you can interact with and learn about.

You can climb aboard ancient locomotive trams, subway cars, train carriages, buses and more, taking you through the ages and confirming for you just how easy it is to take modern transport for granted.

My favourite part of the museum is the old street recreated from 1895 to 1930 that you can meander down, popping in and out of an Edwardian photography studio, a 1930's Italian Café, a 1960's garage, and of course an ol' Glesca pub.

With exhibits floating above your head, and interactive display screens throughout, you'll find it hard to tear yourself away & head out to our dear "Tall Ship", the Glenlee, but make sure you don't miss it; built in this City it went on to circumnavigate the globe 4 times & survive Cape Horn 15 times, and is one of the few core historic UK vessels reflecting the mastery of Clydebuilt technology.

contact

Tel: +44 141 287 2720
Email:
museums@glasgowlife.org.uk

social

glasgowlife.org.uk
facebook.com/riverside.glasgowmuseums
twitter.com/riversidemuseum

when

10am-5pm Mon-Thu & Sat
11am-5pm Fri & Sun

where

100 Pointhouse Place
Glasgow
G3 8RS

WEE GLESCA

A POCKET GUIDE TO GLASGOW

the lighthouse

lowdown

The Lighthouse is Scotland's centre for design & architecture, and for me is one of the most inspiring buildings in the world.

It was the first public commission for one of our favourite sons, Charles Rennie Mackintosh, and you can learn about this amazing man in the Interpretation Centre here. The helical staircase and fantastic 360° view from the top will keep your camera snapping crazily for a while, but throughout the place you'll be held captive by a rich programme of ever changing creative exhibitions, events, markets and educational workshops focusing on Scottish and foreign architecture, digital design, animation and much more.

There's also the MAKLab, which is a 3D digital fabrication laboratory that links with other labs around the country and pushes the envelope in its field.

An absolute masterpiece of a building which hosts absolute masterpieces! Oh, and if that's not enough there's The Doocot on level five, one of my favourite cafés in the City.

contact

Tel: +44 141 276 5360
Email:
information.thelighthouse@glasgow.gov.uk

social

thelighthouse.co.uk
facebook.com/pagcs/the-lighthouse
twitter.com/the_lighthouse

when

10.30am-5pm Mon-Sat
12am-5pm Sun

where

11 Mitchell Lane
Glasgow
G1 3NU

16

top-ten-glasgow-guide.com
facebook.com/toptenglasgowguide
twitter.com/toptenglasgow

WEE GLESCA
A POCKET GUIDE TO GLASGOW

cathedral precinct

lowdown

Along the Cathedral Precinct you'll see our oldest building (Glasgow Cathedral), what's thought to be our oldest house (Provand's Lordship), the St. Mungo Museum of Religion & Visitor Centre, as well as the historically imposing Glasgow Royal Infirmary Hospital, the Barony Church, the Barony North Glasgow Evangelical Church, and our historic High Street which tails off into the delights of Glasgow Green.

Right here you'll learn how our City was born, from the time of our Patron Saint Mungo in the 6th Century, through the 15th Century when the Cathedral was declared by the Pope a place of pilgrimage only Rome could equal, down past the 16th Century when things all went to pot during the murderous Protestant Reformation, and into more recent times as our Second City of the British Empire turned more secular.

It's one of the most fascinating stops on your tour of the City, and your camera will need some serious juice to keep up, particularly in and around the Cathedral which is seen popularly as *the* high point of cathedral construction in Europe.

Make sure to ask your tour guide about sectarianism while you're here, and watch as they get tongue-tied trying to explain it!

contact
Cath Tel: +44 141 552 8198
Cath Email:
info@glasgowcathedral.org.uk
Prov's Tel: 0141 276 1625
Prov's Email:
museums@glasgowlife.org.uk

social
Cathedral:
glasgowcathedral.org.uk
Provand's: glasgowlife.org.uk
Necropolis:
glasgownecropolis.org

when
Varies. Best to check the websites for each attraction.

where
Castle Street
Glasgow
G4 0RB

top-ten-glasgow-guide.com
facebook.com/toptenglasgowguide
twitter.com/toptenglasgow

WEE GLESGA
--•--
A POCKET GUIDE TO GLASGOW
--•--

people's palace & winter gardens

lowdown

This is the place you can learn more about our social history from the 18th Century and onwards, the story of the people of Glasgow. In the myriad of photos, paintings, artefacts, and interactive displays, you can experience what it was like to live here through the ages.

We're often lauded as amongst the most friendly folks on the planet, which could be explained partly as the result of generations of social deprivation and inequality. Through poor health & overcrowding as the City exploded onto the world stage, with the influx of the Irish over time and horrible events like the Calton weavers massacre, our infamous Glesca patter developed together with our unique approach to life and all its laughable social conditioning. In this museum you'll see us through the ages at work, rest & play, at "the Steamie", the single end tenements, "doon the watter", & "at the dancin".

At the fabulous Victorian glasshouse of the Winter Gardens you can also see the world's largest terracotta fountain, the Doulton, and a vast array of tropical plants and flora.

Visiting here will wipe off some of the gloss thrust in your face by the tourist industry, and introduce you to the ordinary, working class folks who made, and still make, this industrious, light-hearted City what she is.

contact
Tel: +44 141 276 0788
Email:
museums@glasgowlife.org.uk

social
glasgowlife.org.uk
facebook.com/peoplespalace.
glasgowmuseums
twitter.com/peoplespalacegl

when
10am-5pm Tue-Thu & Sat
11am-5pm Fri & Sun
10am-5pm All Week Winter Gardens

where
Glasgow Green, Glasgow, G40 1AT

---

top-ten-glasgow-guide.com
facebook.com/toptenglasgowguide
twitter.com/toptenglasgow

WEE GLESCA
A POCKET GUIDE TO GLASGOW

centre for contemporary arts (cca)

lowdown
A seriously cool place! Within Alexander Thomson's Grade A Grecian Chambers lurks one of the main hubs of Glasgow's world famous creative activity.

Other than the brilliant Saramago café bar that I'm prone to frequenting (and not just to convince folks that I'm "bohemian"!), all year you can experience from mainly new & challenging artists some of the planet's most cutting-edge films, music, exhibitions, literature, talks, and festivals. It's gained a reputation as a world class venue for improvised, experimental & electronic music, and plays host each year to various up & coming composers and orchestras.

The place developed from the infamous Third Eye Centre in the 1970s which was described as a "shrine to the *avant garde*" and became the centre for Glasgow counter culture, and since it became the CCA in 1992 its open source curatorial policy that's allowed artists & organisations to propose their own programmes in conjunction with those the

CCA's curated, has continued to cement its place on the global stage.

So if you've a need to be inspired and fancy something different, something you won't experience elsewhere, this is definitely where you should spend some time.

contact
Tel: +44 141 352 4900
Email: gen@cca-glasgow.com

social
cca-glasgow.com
facebook.com/cca.glasgow.1
twitter.com/cca_glasgow

when
10am-midnight Mon-Sat
11am-6pm Tue-Sat
(Galleries)

where
350 Sauchiehall Street
Glasgow
G2 3JD

burrell collection

lowdown

The Burrell is one of the finest examples of why Glasgow just "gets it" when it comes to museums.

Amongst other things, it houses art & artefacts from Ancient Egypt stemming back to 332 B.C.; stunning remnants from Ancient Greece & Rome, gothic reconstructions of Hutton Castle; paintings by Degas, Cézanne & Boudin; Chinese art including fantastic Neolithic burial urns; medieval & religious art; early carpets, rugs and Islamic art; arms & armour from the 13th to 17th centuries; sought-after tapestry galleries; and much, much more.

What's so amazing is that all of this, one of the most extensive collections in the world of its kind, was amassed by just one wee fella fae Glesca with no expertise or deep pockets, and that hey, he simply gave it to us to preserve after he was gone.

It's an outstanding place to take the kids and watch as their eyes dazzle in the astonishment that adults so tragically grow out of. So take the tours, take your time, and take with you forever an experience I have the luxury of repeating over and over again.

Oh, and did I mention that it's situated in Pollok Country Park, voted Europe's best park? A full day's enjoyment from start to finish!

contact
Tel: +44 141 287 2550
Email:
museums@glasgowlife.org.uk

social
glasgowlife.org.uk
facebook.com/theburrellcollection.glasgowmuseums

when
10am-midnight Mon-Thu & Sat
11am-5pm Fri & Sun

where
Pollok Country Park
Pollokshaws Road
Glasgow, G43 1AT

WEE GLESCA
A POCKET GUIDE TO GLASGOW

the mac (glasgow school of art)

lowdown

Despite a horrifying fire in 2014 which led to a period of closure & restoration, this remarkable place remains one of the world's foremost institutions for fine art, design & architecture, and in this city for generations has been at the heart of one of the most influential & creative communities. Designed by Mackintosh, it's lauded as the most seminal building in the country, and the only art school in the world where the building is worthy of the subject.

You can visit and take a breathtaking walking tour of the building itself, or use it as a base to take the Mackintosh tour around the city, renowned as one of the top architectural tours on the planet. Throughout the year there are exhibitions from the students, and it won't take long before you appreciate just how influential it must be learning in a place like this.

Spending some time here, therefore, will give you an unparalleled insight into not only the art nouveau progression in post industrial Glasgow, but also how significant the city has been, and continues to be, on cultural development in Europe and beyond.

All that aside though, at the very least you'll be sure to take away with you some jaw-dropping photos!

contact

Tel: +44 141 353 4500
Tel (Mac tours): +44 141 566 1472
Email: info@gsa.ac.uk

social

gsa.ac.uk
facebook.com/glasgowschoolofart
twitter.com/GSofA

when

Various tours throughout the day, 7 days a week. Visit site for info & to book.

where

167 Renfrew Street
Glasgow
G3 6RQ

the hunterian museum and art gallery

lowdown

Founded in 1807, this is Scotland's oldest public museum, recognised as a Collection of National Significance.

Amongst other fascinating historical nik-naks, you can see here scientific instruments used by the likes of James Watt & Lord Kelvin, Roman artefacts from the Antonine Wall, one of the world's greatest numismatic collections (ie. money!), and ethnographic objects from Captain Cook's voyages in the Pacific.

It also holds the world's largest display of the works of James McNeill Whistler and Charles Rennie Mackintosh, and houses, well, the stunningly recreated house of the latter.

With new temporary exhibitions and collections added throughout every year, you'll wonder why you didn't clear enough time to visit this place. With its public programme increasingly research driven, the museum's historically vital mission in the Age of Enlightenment continues unabated, and it's no wonder why it's still deemed one of Scotland's most important cultural assets.

Oh, and it has a shop!

contact

Tel: +44 141 330 4221
Email: hunterian-enquiries@glasgow.ac.uk

social

gla.ac.uk/hunterian
facebook.com/hunterian-museum-and-art-gallery
twitter.com/hunterian

when

10am-5pm Tue-Sat
11am-4pm Sun
Zoology closed Sat, Sun
Anatomy – by appt only

where

Gilbert Scott Building
University of Glasgow
University Avenue, Glasgow
G12 8QQ

festivals

top-ten-glasgow-guide.com
facebook.com/toptenglasgowguide
twitter.com/toptenglasgow

WEE GLESGA
A POCKET GUIDE TO GLASGOW

celtic connections

lowdown

This is Glasgow's annual folk, roots & world music festival that erupts within the winter darkness and brings the city noisily to life with concerts, ceilidhs, talks, art exhibitions, workshops & free events. It's one of the world's largest winter festivals & the premiere Celtic music festival in the UK.

It's renowned for its strong spirit of collaboration, and it actively promotes cultural exchange between countries throughout the world. Also, at the core of the programme is education, and kids get access to many free morning concerts & events, introducing traditional music, Robert Burns and even blues to young ears used merely to what's hot on iTunes & Spotify (or whatever those wacky young bairns are listening to these days...)!

One of the best parts of the festival to witness is the opening Torchlight Parade, which leads a bustling mass of pipes, drums and flaming torches from George Square to the steps of the Royal Concert Hall. However, the programme is packed, so

make sure you snap up the tickets and sample this unparalleled festival while you're here.

contact

Tel: +44 141 353 8000
Email:
bosales@glasgowconcerthalls.com

social

celticconnections.com
facebook.com/celticconnections
twitter.com/ccfest

when

Over January & early February.
Visit links for events programme.

where

Based at the Glasgow Royal Concert Halls, but events hosted throughout the city.

top-ten-glasgow-guide.com
facebook.com/toptenglasgowguide
twitter.com/toptenglasgow

WEE GLESCA
A POCKET GUIDE TO GLASGOW

glasgow film festival

lowdown

This is an ambitious, fast growing, geek-friendly festival that keeps it "reel" (eh? eh?...) with hundreds of premieres, screenings, panel discussions, live performances & special events around the city showing off the best of Scottish and independent work.

Tickets for the main events sell out like the proverbial hotcakes (I was *hugely* disappointed when I missed the chance to see Joss Whedon here in person!), so keep up with the social media channels & get in there fast.

The festival coincides with the increasingly popular Glasgow Youth Film Festival and the Glasgow Short Film Festival, and regularly innovates by organising unique events including quite recently an absorbing screening in the Glasgow subway network!

It's as popular now as the (supposedly) more famous & industry-delegate-prone one along the road, and given its huge popularity you're more likely than ever now to catch sight of the talented directors, producers, actors & teams behind the most recent successes (box office-wise or not) in the global movie & tv industries.

As a self-confessed film addict, you may have guessed that I heartily recommend this festival!

contact
Tel: +44 141 332 6535
Email:
allisongardner@glasgowfilm.org

social
glasgowfilm.org
facebook.com/glasgowfilmfestival
twitter.com/glasgowfilmfest

when
Over February & March.
Visit links for events programme.

where
Based at GFT (12 Rose St., Glasgow, G3 6RB), but events hosted throughout the city.

25

top-ten-glasgow-guide.com
facebook.com/toptenglasgowguide
twitter.com/toptenglasgow

WEE GLESGA
A POCKET GUIDE TO GLASGOW

international comedy festival

lowdown

The first of its kind in Europe, this festival showcases the major headline comedy acts of the day, the up and coming talents who'd otherwise find it hard to get a look in, and of course the unearthed delights of those in the open mic nights encouraged onto the stage by their mates!

In about 50 venues dotted around the city, you can ache your belly at the best of international comedy, but also find yourself equally chuckled in weirder places like the Glasgow subway or even, if you find it hard to get out without the wee bairns in tow, at a soft play area for an afternoon of comedy for parents.

One of the great things about this festival is the ticket prices. Often you'll find two-for-one deals and low prices, reflecting just how hard the organisers try and introduce to performance comedy those who don't usually spend their hard-earned green at shows and prefer simply to get the DVD at Christmas!

Get in there quick though, as the larger shows are normally sold out as soon as they're on sale.

contact

Tel: +44 141 552 2070
Tel (tickets): 0844 395 4005
Email:
info@glasgowcomedyfestival.com

social

glasgowcomedyfestival.com
facebook.com/glasgowcomedy
twitter.com/glasgowcomedy

when

Over March & April.
Visit links for events programme.

where

Based at 278 High St, Glasgow, G4 0QT, but events hosted throughout the city.

WEE GLESCA
A POCKET GUIDE TO GLASGOW

west end festival

lowdown
Billed as Glasgow's biggest cultural event, this explosion of colour attracts the most vibrant local & international organisations, arts groups & artists to deliver hundreds of activities, projects, events, exhibitions, performances, talks, tours, workshops & screenings, and many are free of charge in over 80 venues to allow accessibility.

The carnival parade at the heart of it all is the largest in the UK outside Notting Hill, and its diversity has been flavoured well by a coupling with the shimmering saris of our Glasgow Mela multicultural festival, and also with the imaginatively inspiring outdoor celebration of Shakespeare that is Bard in the Botanics.

It's just a rich way to bring in the start of the summer, even if it ends up raining, and with the crowds of happy, colourful people dancing in the streets you'll be forgiven for thinking it's the 60s again!

Tickets sell like the proverbial "hot cakes" for this, so get in fast!

contact
Tel: +44 141 341 0844
Email:
info@westendfestival.com

social
westendfestival.com
facebook.com/westendfestival
twitter.com/westendfest

when
Every June.
Visit links for events programme.

where
Events hosted throughout the west end of the city.

WEE GLESCA
A POCKET GUIDE TO GLASGOW

merchant city festival

lowdown

Taking place in my favourite part of the City, this is an absolute flamboyant fiesta of spectacular entertainment.

The Merchant City is home to magnificent architecture, as well as some of the country's finest restaurants, bars, design-led retailers and, obviously, outstanding cultural venues.

Renowned for its ambitious street theatre and outdoor performances & interactive events, the Festival regularly presents an amazing line up including special commissions and premieres as well as music, dance, comedy, visual art, fashion, drama, film, tours, walks, food, markets and a dedicated weekend family zone jam-packed with events and performances to surprise and delight.

A fine addition to the festival for a number of years now has been Vintage, which celebrates the best of British creativity from the 20s onwards, and the unbelievable cabaret of Surge, a festival of circus & street theatre which gets even more bizarrely enjoyable every year.

So wherever you go in the area while it's on you'll be swept up in such a welcoming atmosphere of cultural fun that you won't want it to end!

contact

Tel: +44 141 278 9808
Email:
mcf@glasgowlife.ork.uk

social

merchantcityfestival.com
facebook.com/merchantcityfestival
twitter.com/merchcityfest

when

Over July and August.
Visit links for events programme.

where

Events hosted throughout the Merchant City area of the city.

28

top-ten-glasgow-guide.com
facebook.com/toptenglasgowguide
twitter.com/toptenglasgow

WEE GLESCA
A POCKET GUIDE TO GLASGOW

southside fringe

lowdown
Ok, so how can there be a fringe when there's no festival for it to be a fringe to?!!

For whatever reason the brilliant Southside Festival lost its funding, but thankfully some kindly unrelenting souls in the Southside have kept going the increasingly popular fringe to promote the creative community & its emerging talent, providing entertainment for the diverse locality in a range of fabulous Southside venues.

The team behind it feel that the massive range of arts represented in the Southside deserves its own, dedicated event, and their aim is to provide an experience that includes a wide and diverse range of entertainment for all demographics of the area, aiding economic regeneration & raising the profile of the Southside and its arts landscape, drawing new customers and audiences to the wonderful facilities the Southside has to offer.

Even if you're not from the Southside, make sure you support this wonderful fringe and prove to our esteemed overlords at the Council they were so wrong to pull the funding from the main festival.

contact
Tel: No Tel!
Email:
info@southsidefringe.org.uk

social
southsidefringe.org.uk
facebook.com/southsidefringe
twitter.com/KeepItSouth

when
Every May.
Visit links for events programme.

where
Events hosted throughout the southside area of the city.

top-ten-glasgow-guide.com
facebook.com/toptenglasgowguide
twitter.com/toptenglasgow

WEE GLESCA
A POCKET GUIDE TO GLASGOW

glasgay!

lowdown

This is the largest multi-arts festival of LGBT culture in the UK.

Its ethos is rooted in professional performing, visual arts, and in the highest standards of public engagement. The organisers work with like-minds, sympathetic voices, challenging artists and open-minded, forward-looking institutions to embrace the best of LGBT art & be mindful of social issues.

Over the years Glasgay! has worked with some of the country's leading artists, designers, thinkers and cultural voices, and presents some of the most cutting-edge theatre, visual art, music, dance, comedy, film, literature and exhibitions, over a variety of venues across the City.

Every year it all boils up into a hot debate about identity, sexuality, gender & lifestyle, played out in dramatic contexts that explore, celebrate and raise the profile of LGBT life in the world today.

Despite how much has progressed since the festival's inception, many in the LGBT community here still struggle with mental health, family issues and identity crises, so high profile events like this do make a difference. As Sir Ian McKellen once uttered, "Glasgay! is a beacon of sanity in a hypocritical and naughty world".

contact
Tel: +44 141 552 7575
Email: info@glasgay.com

social
glasgay.co.uk
facebook.com/glasgay
twitter.com/glasgayfestival

when
Mid-October to mid-November.
Visit links for events programme.

where
Events hosted throughout the centre and west end of the city.

---

top-ten-glasgow-guide.com
facebook.com/toptenglasgowguide
twitter.com/toptenglasgow

30

WEE GLESCA
A POCKET GUIDE TO GLASGOW

gi festival

lowdown

Glasgow International Festival of Visual Art is a world-renowned biennial festival of contemporary art. It is famous for providing the UK's most balanced showcase of the best of local and international art for wide-ranging audiences, and takes place in various venues and locations across the City, including Glasgow's major art spaces and cultural institutions, with sought-after and often as yet unseen exhibitions, installations, sculptures, multi-media events, talks, projects & even stand-up comedy by international and Glasgow-based artists.

Although all at once it might seem overwhelming, it always proves to be rich, dense, organic and inspiring. To be fair though, you wouldn't expect any less from the City that's heralded consistently for outperforming any other place in the UK for creativity and contemporary art. The festival provides the heartbeat for the ongoing "Glasgow Miracle", which day in day out continues to push the boundaries in art and sweep to one side the lazy, indoctrinated stereotype painted so tiresomely of the City.

It's only a shame that we don't have it every year!

contact
Tel: +44 141 276 8384
Email:
info@glasgowinternational.org

social
glasgowinternational.org
facebook.com/gifestival
twitter.com/gifestival

when
Biennial on even years, April to May. Visit links for events programme.

where
Events hosted throughout pretty much every area in the city.

31

top-ten-glasgow-guide.com
facebook.com/toptenglasgowguide
twitter.com/toptenglasgow

A POCKET GUIDE TO GLASGOW

aye write!

lowdown

Aye Write! is Glasgow's Book Festival taking place in the stunning Mitchell Library, one of Europe's largest public libraries and one of Glasgow's most iconic landmarks since it opened in 1911.

The festival celebrates the best in national, international and local writing, and annually brings an eclectic array of national and local speakers to the library, allowing audiences to enjoy appearances from big name writers as well as emerging talent.

The programme includes a wide range of ticketed celebrity author events for adults and children, but also extends to a brilliant schools festival called Wee Write!, and a variety of free community and family events, creative writing workshops

While you're in the library you will have the opportunity of exploring not only the way in which literary works continue to educate, inspire & transform in a world so readily distracted culturally, but you can also take some time to explore your ancestry and the roots of the City bursting out of its massive records section.

Will you learn something interesting at this festival? Aye right!

contact

Tel: +44 141 287 2999
Email:
ayewrite@glasgowlife.org.uk

social

ayewrite.com
facebook.com/ayewrite
twitter.com/ayewrite

when

Every April. Visit links for events programme. Wee Write! every March.

where

Mitchell Library
Glasgow, G3 7DN

WEE GLESCA
A POCKET GUIDE TO GLASGOW

glasgow science festival

lowdown
This is now one of the largest science festivals in the UK. GSF takes memorable events to non-traditional venues across the City where geekly cool lovers of science engage with thousands of people from all ages and backgrounds, from novices to experts, to showcase the outstanding contribution our City & her researchers make to the worlds of science, technology, engineering, maths and medicine.

The list of Scottish innovation in science is pretty long. Logarithms, electromagnetism, the Higgs boson, discovery of many stars & galaxies, oil refinery, the incandescent light bulb, the Kelvin unit of temperature, criminal fingerprinting, the first cloned mammal. Like I say, pretty long, and a festival like this can help you tap into why our country is so full of wizard mad creativity in science.

You can explore everything from astronomy to zoology through art, comedy, film, workshops and interactive fun in laboratories. So all you Big Bang Theory fans out there with your wacky t-shirts (yes, I'm one of them!), get your science on in Glasgow and be inspired.

contact
Tel: +44 141 330 5370
Email: sciencefestival@glasgow.ac.uk

social
glasgowsciencefestival.org.uk
facebook.com/glasgowscience festival
twitter.com/glasgowscifest

when
Every June. Visit links for events programme.

where
Events hosted in various venues throughout the city.

restaurants

WEE GLESCA

A POCKET GUIDE TO GLASGOW

grill on the corner

lowdown

Much as in any other town you'll hear of steakhouses hailing themselves, or being hailed, as serving THE best steak. You'll hear other quality joints being dismissed as inferior. And after hearing all this you might decide to favour one place over another, again and again.

Well, all I can say in the face of that is: don't listen to nowt but your own gut. I can only go by mine, and mine tells me that THE best steakhouse in Glasgow is the Grill on the Corner. And it tells me this having experienced pretty much all the steakhouses in Glasgow.

So am I right about this? Who knows. Your gut might tell you something else, maybe even that you don't like steak (heavens above!), but if you do like steak and never tried Kobe or Wagyu, which really is the daddy of all steak, then at least let your gut make an informed choice and learn why I wax nothing short of lyrical about it on the site.

Oh, and other than the array of cuts available, the rest of the menu is pretty outstanding, so get yersel o'er pronto!

contact
Tel: +44 141 248 6262
Email:
grillonthecorner@blackhouse.uk.com

social
blackhouse.uk.com/glasgow
facebook.com/grillonthecorner.glasgow
twitter.com/glasgowgrill

when
11am-12am Mon-Sat
11am-11pm Sun

where
21-25 Bothwell Street
Glasgow
G2 6NL

35

top-ten-glasgow-guide.com
facebook.com/toptenglasgowguide
twitter.com/toptenglasgow

WEE GLESGA
A POCKET GUIDE TO GLASGOW

red onion

lowdown
In recent years as Glasgow's found her confidence in this mad culinary world where, so it's said, only Michelin matters, there's been a burgeoning array of cutting edge gourmet restaurants entering the scene here oozing total cool. To be fair, I love most of them.

However, when restaurants stand the test of time while retaining that initial new kid on the block veneer, I get the impression they must be pretty special.

Red Onion has been a fixture in my top ten since I started the site. Owner John Quigley used to be private chef to the likes of Guns n' Roses, and to this day he continues to bring rock and roll to his eclectically superb menu.

One of my personal favourites here has been the Moroccan spiced braised lamb shoulder with apricot & almond tagine, bejewelled cous cous and tzatziki salad, and there's plenty more of that level of quality on display, particularly in the innovative Scottish dishes.

A nice, relaxing & friendly way to start your evening before the theatre or to end it after a hard day's shopping.

contact
Tel: +44 141 221 6000
Email: info@red-onion.co.uk

social
red-onion.co.uk
facebook.com/redonionglasgow
twitter.com/redonionglasgow

when
12noon-late Sun-Sat

where
257 West Campbell Street
Glasgow
G2 4TT

top-ten-glasgow-guide.com
facebook.com/toptenglasgowguide
twitter.com/toptenglasgow

WEE GLESGA
A POCKET GUIDE TO GLASGOW

two fat ladies & gamba

lowdown

Two Fat Ladies & Gamba are for me the joint best places in the City to sample the world famous delights of the Scottish waters.

For TFL I still prefer the Blythswood restaurant over the ones in the West End or at the Buttery, but having tried each regularly you don't have to worry if one's nearer than the others, as the quality in each is unparalleled.

There are plenty of fine fish restaurants in Glasgow, but with fresh immaculate dishes between these two like seared scallops with stornoway black pudding & sweetcorn puree, and swordfish with celeriac remoulade, courgette puree & fried whitebait; Isle of Gigha halibut, pan-fried, Brown shrimps, capers, almonds, parsley, lemon; and roast Shetland Cod, creamed cabbage, pancetta, peas, mussels and thyme, you might begin to understand why I keep returning like a leaping salmon year in year out.

The feeling I get from these places every time I step into their underwater-themed cosiness is just warming, and even though I end up completely stuffed I always come out wanting more.

contact

TFL Tel: +44 141 847 0088
Email:
mailto:city@twofatladiesresta urant.com
Gamba Tel: +44 141 572 0899
Email: info@gamba.co.uk

social

twofatladiesrestaurant.com/c itycentre
facebook.com/two-fat-ladies-city-centre
twitter.com/twofatladies88
gamba.co.uk
facebook.com/gambaglasgow
twitter.com/gamba_glasgow

when

12pm-3pm Mon-Sat
5.30pm-10.30pm Mon-Sat
1pm-9pm Sun

where

TFL 118A Blythswood Street, Glasgow, G2 4EG
Gamba 225a W. George St., Glasgow, G2 2ND

37

top-ten-glasgow-guide.com
facebook.com/toptenglasgowguide
twitter.com/toptenglasgow

WEE GLESGA
-o-
A POCKET GUIDE TO GLASGOW
-oo-

don costanzo's

lowdown

Costanzo Cacace carved an unforgettable slice of Caprese into the fabric of Glasgow when he opened Ristorante Caprese on Buchanan Street.

When that had to close in the face of relentless retail development in the City Centre, despite a looooong court case, Costanzo and his family simply upped sticks and re-opened along the road, much to the relief of many sad friends and patrons.

I can't get enough of the pure authenticity I feel when I walk through the doors to his place. It's more an experience spending time here than it is a meal. You'll be left alone if you like, but given the atmosphere of collective fun pulsing around you, it won't take long before you want to be a part of it, laughing and singing, never wanting to leave!

The food there is, of course, exquisite, with dishes like scaloppina pizzaiola, spaghetti salsicce, and filetto di Manzo, although I recommend that you listen carefully to the specials Costanzo lays out for you, as I've never been disappointed.

THE best Italian restaurant in town, bar none!

contact
Tel: +44 141 332 3070
Email:
mailto:jomcgilp@yahoo.com

social
doncostanzo.com
facebook.com/don-costanzo
twitter.com/doncostanzos

when
Varied hours, check site for details

where
13 Woodside Crescent
Glasgow
G3 7UL

top-ten-glasgow-guide.com
facebook.com/toptenglasgowguide
twitter.com/toptenglasgow

WEE GLESCA
A POCKET GUIDE TO GLASGOW

the dhabba

lowdown

The Dhabba (or 'diner' in Punjabi) is held out as one of the most authentic North Indian restaurants in the UK. I just can't get enough of the place and her South Indian sister Dakhin along the cobbled road in the Merchant City.

Put to one side the stodge and food colourings of the usual level of Indian you might normally expect in these here parts, and tuck into some dishes of sheer excellence you'll be talking about for years.

Choose from the likes of Boti Kabab Badami, Haryali Murg Tikka, Mili Juli Sabzi Seekh, a choice of ancient sauces like Maskawala & Palakdaar, head for the slow-cooked Dum Pukht selection including the mouth-watering Jheenga Dum Nisha or Murg Khusk Purdah, or dive into the ocean with Machi Begum Bahar.

From that example of choice you'll guess that this absolute mastery of a restaurant will raise your expectations and appreciation of fine Indian cooking.

There are many outstanding Indian restaurants in Glasgow, but having tried most of them I'm afraid the Dhabba's never been knocked off the top spot for me!

contact
Tel: +44 141 553 1249
Email:
mailto:info@thedhabba.com

social
thedhabba.com
facebook.com/thedhabba
twitter.com/thedhabba

when
12noon-2pm Mon-Fri
5pm-11pm Mon-Fri
1pm-11pm Sat-Sun

where
44 Candleriggs
Glasgow
G1 1LE

WEE GLESCA
A POCKET GUIDE TO GLASGOW

khublai khans mongolian barbecue

lowdown

Possibly the most fun you'll have eating out in Glasgow!

At Khublai Khans, the Mongolian barbeque feast idea, inspired by the 13th century Mongol warriors, is that you have a starter, then grab a bowl, fire in some rice or noodles, put some of the huge array of meats & seafood in that bowl (including anything from springbok to shark!), then some veg, and then spoon or pour in whatever herbs, oils, sauces and spices you feel like to create your own dish which is then grilled before your eyes. And then you do it again. And again!

You can follow the menus on the wall if you like, or just fire it all in and see what you end up with. However you create your dishes though, you'll end up chatting with everyone in your group and even random strangers about what they're putting in theirs, so it always ends up being a superb way to break the ice and enjoy a dining out experience you'll never forget.

If you can fit it in, make sure you try the Ulan Gad for dessert!

contact

Tel: +44 141 552 5646
Email:
glasgow@khublaikhan.co.uk

social

khublaikhan-glasgow.co.uk
facebook.com/khublaikhans
twitter.com/khublaikhans

when

5pm-11pm Sun-Thu
12noon-12pm Fri-Sat

where

26 Candleriggs
Glasgow
G1 1LD

top-ten-glasgow-guide.com
facebook.com/toptenglasgowguide
twitter.com/toptenglasgow

WEE GLESCA
A POCKET GUIDE TO GLASGOW

tony roma's at xscape

lowdown
I've been absolutely 'ribbed' for including this place in my top ten for years.

This world famous rib joint apparently isn't cool, trendy and refined enough to make it into a list of the best places to dine out in Glasgow. So as you can imagine, I had no difficulty including it again in this guide!

I can't help it if I enjoy slow-cooked ribs coated in smoky barbeque sauce. It's a personal choice, and rather like my fingers after eating here, I'm sticking to it! I still drool at the thought of heading here, as it takes me right back to the US where Tracey and I have spent a fair few years travelling. So it ain't Scottish, it ain't pretty, but for me it definitely ain't something to be missed.

I doubt a fancier place would be appreciated as much anyway given its location in the thrill-a-minute sanctuary of Soar (formerly XScape), as it's a classic way to regain some energy after some time on the slopes or climbing those rocks.

Finger-lickin' good!

contact
Tel: +44 141 886 8630
Email:
enquiries@tonyromas.co.uk

social
tonyromas.co.uk
facebook.comtonyromasuk
twitter.com/tonyromasuk

when
12noon-10pm Mon-Thu
12noon-11pm Fri-Sat
12noon-10.30pm Sun

where
Soar at intu Braehead
Kings Inch Road
Braehead
Renfrew, PA4 8XQ

41

top-ten-glasgow-guide.com
facebook.com/toptenglasgowguide
twitter.com/toptenglasgow

panda chinese cuisine

lowdown

Again, another one I've taken some slack for including in my top ten list. To that I say "go and do your own list then, smarty pants"!

Panda's been on my radar for years now, and you'd normally expect standards to slip a little as the years roll on, or for the uniqueness of such a place to be surpassed by something new, somewhere just better.

But here it is, still the place to go for a Chinese buffet in Glasgow. As I say on the site, there's a myriad of fabulous, authentic Oriental restaurants in the City that I sample as much as I can, but for a 'totes gorge' experience on a night out with mates, I head here and start the night with a bang bang!

Great place to go before the bowling or heading into town, and also a brilliant place for a takeaway if you're just heading indoors.

contact

Tel: +44 141 429 0988
Email:
panda.cuisine@btconnect.com

social

pandacuisine.co.uk
facebook.com/pages/panda-chinese-cuisine
twitter.com/panda_cuisine

when

11.30am-11pm Mon-Sat
11am-11pm Sun

where

Springfield Quay
Glasgow
G5 8NP

top-ten-glasgow-guide.com
facebook.com/toptenglasgowguide
twitter.com/toptenglasgow

WEE GLESCA
A POCKET GUIDE TO GLASGOW

the sisters (kelvingrove)

lowdown

As I say on the site, out of the two Sisters restaurants in the City, my old favourite is still the one in Kelvingrove. Strictly speaking it's actually located in the Finnieston area of the City, which in recent years has been rivalling the Southside as the most 'up and coming' place to be in Glasgow.

If you're heading to a gig at the Hydro or simply thinking of a chilled out night out in the area, here's one of the best places to start the evening.

For me it remains the top Scots restaurant in Glasgow. Run by (now celebrity) chef Jacqueline O'Donnell, she's laid out a wonderful set up in the place that makes you feel like you're dining at home with friends, and designed a stunning menu which makes the best of Scottish produce. Wild Highland venison loin with Arran beetroot & red cabbage slaw and Tayside raspberry balsamic glaze. Slow baked Ramsay's of Carluke ham with scallion mashed rooster tatties &

whisky and Arran mustard sauce. Puff candy meringue with honeycomb ice cream, meringue & homemade marshmallow sundae.

Absolute perfection!

contact
Tel: +44 141 564 1157
Email: e.jak@thesisters.co.uk

social
thesisters.co.uk
facebook.com/pages-the-sisters-kelvingrove
twitter.com/chef_jacqueline

when
12noon-9.15pm Mon-Sat
12noon-8.30pm Sun

where
36 Kelvingrove Street
Glasgow
G3 7RZ

top-ten-glasgow-guide.com
facebook.com/toptenglasgowguide
twitter.com/toptenglasgow

WEE GLESGA
A POCKET GUIDE TO GLASGOW

malaga tapas

lowdown

You'll find that there are a great many Spanish restaurants in Glasgow. Without a shadow of doubt this hidden gem in the Southside is the only one I see as being totally authentic.

The owner Cristobal used to work in the Battlefield Rest, one of my favourite *Italian* restaurants in the City, but I don't think many folks here who've been lucky enough to find this amazing place and sampled its delights regret his decision some years ago to strike out on his own and, in not exactly the best location in town, create something magical from his own background.

The menu is influenced heavily by Andalucia in the 7th century. I've been there slightly more recently than that, and stepping into this wee place thousands of miles from the dense mountains of Sierra Morena, you'd be forgiven for thinking you're somewhere else.

Tracey's favourite is the croquetas de pollo, mine is the gambas gabardina. The entire menu is filled with more of the same and the feeling you get just by sitting there, breathing in the familial atmosphere, will leave you checking your diary for the next free night to return!

contact

Tel: +44 141 429 4604
Email:
info@malagatapas.co.uk

social

malagatapas.co.uk
facebook.com/pages/malaga-tapas
twitter.com/tapasmalaga

when

12noon-2.30pm Mon-Sat
5pm-10pm Mon-Sat
5pm-10pm Sun

where

213-215 St. Andrew's Road
Glasgow
G41 1PD

44

top-ten-glasgow-guide.com
facebook.com/toptenglasgowguide
twitter.com/toptenglasgow

mackintosh buildings

top-ten-glasgow-guide.com
facebook.com/toptenglasgowguide
twitter.com/toptenglasgow

WEE GLESCA

A POCKET GUIDE TO GLASGOW

the mac (glasgow school of art)

lowdown

Despite a horrifying fire in 2014 which led to a period of closure & restoration, this remarkable place remains one of the world's foremost institutions for fine art, design & architecture, and in this city for generations has been at the heart of one of the most influential & creative communities. Designed by Mackintosh, it's lauded as the most seminal building in the country, and the only art school in the world where the building is worthy of the subject.

You can visit and take a breathtaking walking tour of the building itself, or use it as a base to take the Mackintosh tour around the city, renowned as one of the top architectural tours on the planet. Throughout the year there are exhibitions from the students, and it won't take long before you appreciate just how influential it must be learning in a place like this.

Spending some time here, therefore, will give you an unparalleled insight into not only the art nouveau progression in post industrial Glasgow, but also how significant the city has been, and continues to be, on cultural development in Europe and beyond.

All that aside though, at the very least you'll be sure to take away with you some jaw-dropping photos!

contact

Tel: +44 141 353 4500
Tel (Mac tours): +44 141 566 1472
Email: info@gsa.ac.uk

social

gsa.ac.uk
facebook.com/glasgowschool ofart
twitter.com/GSofA

when

Various tours throughout the day, 7 days a week. Visit site for info & to book.

where

167 Renfrew Street
Glasgow
G3 6RQ

top-ten-glasgow-guide.com
facebook.com/toptenglasgowguide
twitter.com/toptenglasgow

WEE GLESGA

A POCKET GUIDE TO GLASGOW

mackintosh house

lowdown

This is an inch-perfect recreation of Mackintosh's house at 78 Southpark Avenue, the original of which was just down the road.

Same dimensions, same exploration of light & cutting edge design, with the exact colour schemes, fabric, furniture. You're seeing exactly what the great man himself would have seen as he walked around his gaff in the 1900s, settling in to read the Sunday newspaper!

This stunning effect is made all the more delightful when you take a look at the stark and disembodied contrast of the outside of the building, with its front door hanging suspended above the ground without any stairs leading up to it, and the whole façade merging so closely with the University building that you'd be forgiven for not noticing it as you walked on by.

It might just be a wee hoose, but we're pretty lucky to have it in the neighbourhood!

contact

Tel: +44 141 330 4221
Email: hunterian-enquiries@glasgow.ac.uk

social

gla.ac.uk/hunterian/
facebook.com/Hunterian-Museum
twitter.com/hunterian

when

10am-5pm Tues-Sat
11am-4pm Sun

where

University of Glasgow
University Avenue
Glasgow, G12 8QQ

top-ten-glasgow-guide.com
facebook.com/toptenglasgowguide
twitter.com/toptenglasgow

WEE GLESCA
A POCKET GUIDE TO GLASGOW

willow tea rooms

lowdown

The great thing about this place is that you could be shopping your heart out in the City Centre, your mind filled only with bargain buys & queue jumping, yet when you pop into the Willow Tea Rooms for a bite to eat or a refreshing drink, in a flash you're transported to a polite, bygone age, decorated in luxurious artistic symmetry which makes you forget for a while the need to rush around.

My stomach tells me that it's the best of all Charles Rennie Mackintosh buildings because you can tuck into a fine menu of delights like cullen skink, haggis or a St. Andrew's Platter, or you can even sip your way like a Lord or Lady through an afternoon tea & scones, in opulent surroundings that belie the absorbing consumerism reaking turmoil on the street outside.

Other than the menu though, the Willow was the only tea room building in which Mackintosh had 100% control over every part of its design, and his influence shines through each window, every piece of furniture, glass and cutlery, leaving you with a complete appreciation of what he himself wanted to feel when he sat there for his tea break!

Take your time to explore the Room de Luxe and the Gallery, two rooms which spring from the same mind but completely contradict each other, and I can guarantee that when you step back out into the hustle of Sauchiehall Street, you'll be feeling slightly more relaxed and refined than you did when you went in - putting aside that this is one of those jewel in the crown Charles Rennie Mackintosh buildings, at the end of the day you just can't beat a great cup of tea!

contact
Tel: +44 141 332 0521 & +44 141 204 5242 (Buchanan)
Email:
willowtearooms.co.uk/contact-us/

social
willowtearooms.co.uk/
facebook.com/willowtearooms/
twitter.com/willowtearooms

when
9am-5pm Mon-Sat
11am-5pm Sun

where
217 Sauchiehall Street
Glasgow, G2 3EX &
97 Buchanan Street
Glasgow, G1 3HF

WEE GLESCA
A POCKET GUIDE TO GLASGOW

ruchill church hall

lowdown

This is one of the lesser known Charles Rennie Mackintosh buildings, and was designed originally for the Wee Free, our colloquial name for the Free Church of Scotland.

It's a relatively simple two-story building fleshed out with the usual Mackintosh trimmings, and is used every day by an active congregation so I'd recommend being respectful to the locals using the place.

You'll find there a few committee rooms and a Mackintosh Tearoom, but the big draw has to be the main hall pictured here, and given the time and effort Mackintosh put into its design and construction, you may well end up with the impression as I get that it looks quite distractingly out of place amongst the area of Ruchill surrounding the hall, without its effect being diminished.

My personal favourite here however, is the open passageway between the hall and the church adjoining it, as if you stand just inside the doorway, it opens up a chance for you to take without any effort an architectural photo professional enough to land itself on the pages of any gallery!

It really is the case that every one of the Charles Rennie Mackintosh buildings in Glasgow are designed so intricately, that taking photos from any angle will end up impressing your friends & family, unless of course you ruin the moment by standing in front of the camera with a cheesy smile on your face!

contact
Tel: +44 141 946 0466
Email:
enquiries@ruchillparish.org.uk

social
ruchillparish.org.uk/

when
Check website for sermons & events

where
15-17 Shakespeare Street
Glasgow, G20 8TH

49

top-ten-glasgow-guide.com
facebook.com/toptenglasgowguide
twitter.com/toptenglasgow

WEE GLESGA
A POCKET GUIDE TO GLASGOW

queen's cross church

lowdown

When my interest in Charles Rennie Mackintosh buildings was first kindled, I was completely flummoxed that in his lifetime he'd only ever designed and had built one church, the modern gothic Queens Cross Church in Maryhill.

However, the more I looked into it, the more apparent it became that given the artistic latitude offered to Mackintosh on other projects, and the resulting (and sometimes controversial) flair of his work, the stricter and more conventional attitude of the various religious institutions had ensured that he'd never been commissioned for more churches.

That's a shame though, because taking a browse in and around the Queens Cross Church, you may begin to appreciate just how appropriately his designs go hand in hand with the conflict of solemnity & gloriousness you'd expect in a church.

I may say that this is one of the least visited Charles Rennie Mackintosh buildings, even though it's the international HQ of the CRM Society, and reveals to you some astounding examples of Mackintosh's mastery in stained glass and his ornately carved wood & stone work. The last time that I popped along to see it I was the only person there, and believe it or not I had to ring the bell and wait about 5 minutes before the curator finally opened the door and let me in!

Quite astonishing given the sights I was privy to once I walked around the place, and I'd certainly recommend that if the same happens to you when you visit, a little patience will be richly rewarded (although don't go there on a Saturday as I'm pretty sure it's closed).

contact
Tel: +44 141 946 6600
Email: info@crmsociety.com

social
mackintoshchurch.com
facebook.com/mackintosh-queens-cross
twitter.com/mackqueenscross

when
Check website for events & open days

where
870 Garscube Road,
Glasgow, G20 7EL

top-ten-glasgow-guide.com
facebook.com/toptenglasgowguide
twitter.com/toptenglasgow

WEE GLESGA
A POCKET GUIDE TO GLASGOW

martyrs' public school

lowdown

This is one of the earliest Charles Rennie Mackintosh buildings, and was built on the same street Mackintosh himself was born on.

To be perfectly honest, if you come to this school looking for the delicate and distinctive motifs normally associated with the man, you might be a little disappointed, because in designing this place Mackintosh had in mind more in the way of utility rather than impressive decoration.

The reason you shouldn't ignore this as a great Glasgow attraction however, is that it gives you a deeper insight into the flowing timeline of Mackintosh's work and inspiration, being one of his first forays into art nouveau, and because in the organic woodwork and tiling inside, it still reflects his desire to break the mould and sculpt a new, unique artistry.

If anything, it's a brilliant stop if you're doing a tour of the High Street, and deserves

its place of pride amongst all the other Charles Rennie Mackintosh buildings in the continual preservation of Glasgow's memory.

contact

Tel: +44 141 946 6600
Email: info@crmsociety.com

social

glasgowmackintosh.com/attraction/martyrs-school

when

The school is not open to the public, but can be admired from the outside at any time!

where

Parson Street,
Glasgow, G4 0PX

51

top-ten-glasgow-guide.com
facebook.com/toptenglasgowguide
twitter.com/toptenglasgow

WEE GLESGA
A POCKET GUIDE TO GLASGOW

the lighthouse

lowdown

Of all the Charles Rennie Mackintosh buildings, this, the former head office of the Glasgow Herald newspaper, is a structure which brings delight looking out as well as within. It's the internationally trumpeted home of Scotland's Centre for Architecture, Design and the City, and whilst there's some underground controversy in these parts about how much funding this place gets in comparison with other similar projects all around Scotland, as a visitor you can put all that to one side and simply appreciate just how exciting a venue the Lighthouse is, given just how much time, effort and hard cash has been pumped into it.

Take some tourist time to snap some sparkling photos of the wonderfully captivating spiral staircase (be careful when you're leaning over the banister!), the 360° rooftop panorama view and from the outside, the majesty of the building itself as it shoots unfettered into the sky. I'd suggest though, that if you really want to experience the life and effect of Mackintosh without heaving your way through some book, just put the camera away for a while and breathe in the insightful Mackintosh Interpretation, and all the interactive and genuinely enthralling exhibits, workshops & seminars peppered around the building, before resting your mind and your weary legs in The Doocot, the ultra modern café on the 5th floor with its cutting-edge design and well-coveted gnocci (yeah there's a surprise Docherty - it always comes down to the food!).

To get a better flavour of what'll be on when you visit, I'd recommend the official site, but as I always conclude no matter what I'm on about when it comes to the best Glasgow attractions, the most fruitful way of approaching this gaff is simply to open your mind and enjoy it when you get there.

contact
Tel: +44 141 276 5360
Email:
information.thelighthouse@glasgow.gov.uk

social
thelighthouse.co.uk
facebook.com/pages/the-lighthouse
twitter.com/the_lighthouse

when
10.30am-5pm Mon-Sat
12am-5pm Sun

where
11 Mitchell Lane
Glasgow
G1 3NU

top-ten-glasgow-guide.com
facebook.com/toptenglasgowguide
twitter.com/toptenglasgow

WEE GLESCA
A POCKET GUIDE TO GLASGOW

daily record building (stereo)

lowdown
Today the Daily Record Building houses an indie cool vegetarian café, bar & gig venue called Stereo, but whilst it is a pretty funky place to hang out, for me an historic building like this deserves a great deal more in the way of rejuvenation. Before Stereo opened, it had stood for too long as nothing but a tragic shell, hidden away in a poorly lit lane, kind of like the forgotten ornament in your loft or garage, gradually attracting the creeping dust of abandonment

And believe me, it really is nothing but a crying shame, because for a City that spends so much time telling everyone how proud we are of our history, to take an electrifying tour of all these internationally famous Charles Rennie Mackintosh buildings, it beggars belief that absolutely no public funds have been made available to reinvigorate this one, particularly when you consider just how magnificently important the Daily Record building and its vital streams of news became to our ancestors during WWII.

Still, you can revel in the white glazed brick and the stylised Tree of Life motifs adorning the walls, contrasting with the shadows depriving the surrounding buildings of light, and you can eye a few alternative gigs after a decent meal there, and though I'd just love it if I could walk inside and take a look around a meticulous restoration of its inner workings, I reckon that the only alternative is to shout from the rooftops about why this brilliant piece of our artistic development, one of the most instrumental of all the Charles Rennie Mackintosh buildings, deserves just a little bit more of our attention.

contact
Tel: +44 141 946 6600
Email: info@crmsociety.com

social
glasgowmackintosh.com/attraction/daily-record-building

when
Only the groundfloor is open to the public as Stereo cafe, whose hours vary.

where
20-26 Renfield Lane
Glasgow, G2 5AT

top-ten-glasgow-guide.com
facebook.com/toptenglasgowguide
twitter.com/toptenglasgow

WEE GLESGA
A POCKET GUIDE TO GLASGOW

scotland street school museum

lowdown

Making your way into and around the Scotland Street School Museum, you'll witness first hand how differently our children were educated throughout the Victorian era, WWII and up to the 60's. You can actually walk around with your guides (the Jannie, the Heidie & the Teach - it'll all make sense when you get there!) in perfectly restored classrooms, the cloakrooms in which friendships were formed & fights broken up, and use cutting-edge interactive technology to learn all about the developing methods of teaching and discipline in Scotland, and the forgotten games won & lost in the playground over the years.

You'll be able to hear & read the recollections of school pupils, and even sit in on a re-enacted lesson conducted in a scarily formal classroom (I'd be careful about this one though - it has the tendency to make you feel again like the child you outgrew years ago, as it reinvigorates your own fond memories of playing the fool in class or building up the courage to ask someone out!...).

However, all this won't make you forget that at the end of the day, this is one of those jaw-dropping Charles Rennie Mackintosh buildings you should visit at least once in your life, and everywhere you look you'll see his designs integrate into the character of the school, creating the type and level of institutional enlightenment experienced by students every day in the Glasgow School of Art.

Just imagine what it would've been like to be a pupil there!

contact
Tel: +44 141 287 0500
Email:
museums@glasgowlife.org.uk

social
glasgowlife.org.uk
facebook.com/ScotlandStreet
School.GlasgowMuseums
twitter.comglasgowmuseums

when
10am-5pm Tues-Thu, Sat
11am-5pm Fri & Sun

where
225 Scotland Street
Glasgow, G5 8QB

top-ten-glasgow-guide.com
facebook.com/toptenglasgowguide
twitter.com/toptenglasgow

WEE GLESGA
--•--
A POCKET GUIDE TO GLASGOW
--•--

house for an art lover

lowdown

The designs for this breathtaking piece of artistry emanated from a wee German architecture competition from which Mackintosh had been disqualified (in typical Scots fashion he'd submitted his entry after the deadline!).

The rooms in this place really are so astounding that even with a good thesaurus and a direct line to Shakespeare, my words couldn't do them justice. All I'll say is that if you're pressed for time and don't know which of the Charles Rennie Mackintosh buildings to visit, put this one smack bang at the top of your list. It's always busy here, and as well as the unforgettable visionary designs & architecture on display, if you plan your visit well you might be lucky to enjoy one of the feisty music recitals or dinner concerts they put on, after you've spent some quality time in the Art Lovers' Café & Shop or in one of the outstanding art exhibitions organised regularly.

I'm really not kidding when I say that this place is so absorbing, so inspirational even for folks who know nothing about design & architecture, that writing about it may well diminish your anticipation. Just clear an afternoon, go there, amble around with an open mind, and send me your photos and thoughts (after experiencing the sheer wonder of the House for an Art Lover, my favourite of all the Charles Rennie Mackintosh buildings, I'll expect nothing short of sonnets and poetry from you!).

contact
Tel: +44 141 353 4770
Email:
enquiries@houseforanartlover.co.uk

social
houseforanartlover.co.uk/
facebook.com/pages/House-for-an-Art-Lover/
twitter.com/HouseArtLover

when
Varies throughout the year, check website for details.

where
Bellahouston Park
10 Dumbreck Road
Glasgow, G41 5BW

top-ten-glasgow-guide.com
facebook.com/toptenglasgowguide
twitter.com/toptenglasgow

WEE GLESGA
A POCKET GUIDE TO GLASGOW

attractions

top-ten-glasgow-guide.com
facebook.com/toptenglasgowguide
twitter.com/toptenglasgow

WEE GLESCA

A POCKET GUIDE TO GLASGOW

kelvingrove art gallery & museum

lowdown

One of THE most visited attractions in the country, the Kelvingrove hosts our largest civic collection, with 22 state-of-the-art galleries & over 8,000 spectacular items of natural history, arms & armour, art and much more.

I can't get enough of this place. Its Spanish Baroque architecture is stunning, the massive halls breathtaking, but if you see anything here I'd make sure you catch the looming LA198 Spitfire, Sir Rodger the Asian Elephant, the Sarcophagus of PaBaSa, Dali's Christ of St. John on the Cross, and Van Gogh's portrait of Alexander Reid.

There's just so much to see and do (particularly for kids, interactive workshops, study & discovery centres abound!), that you really need to set aside at least a few hours and visit for yourself. You might even be lucky to hear the resounding acoustics of the massive Grade One organ which plays regularly throughout the day.

contact

Tel: +44 141 276 9500
Email:
museums@glasgowlife.org.uk

social

glasgowlife.org.uk
facebook.com/kelvingrove.gla
sgowmuseums
twitter.com/kelvingroveart

when

10am-5pm Mon-Thu
11am-5pm Fri & Sun

where

Argyle Street
Glasgow
G83 8AG

top-ten-glasgow-guide.com
facebook.com/toptenglasgowguide
twitter.com/toptenglasgow

WEE GLESCA
A POCKET GUIDE TO GLASGOW

the mackintosh ten

lowdown

As you may have noticed with my section on Mackintosh, I'm a fan.

After poking around these breathtaking buildings, I'll lay out some green that you will be too!

If you have the time when you're here, make sure you grab a Mackintosh trail ticket and head to as many of the ten as you can. You don't have to know much about architecture - Once you've delved into the soul of these structures, captured how his distinctive motifs and shapes appear to drift their way through every brick, every table and chair, just take a walk around Glasgow after that, and try to see if you notice the Mackintosh blueprint nestling behind anything else, whether it's in the fabric of a building, the theme of a restaurant, even in the glass of busy shop windows and the jewellery behind them.

It won't take long before you notice that the dynamic work he bequeathed us, his art nouveau hunger for artistic revolution, has integrated our way of life to such an extent that it's moulded over the years into a stimulating pulse that beats under everything Glasgow aspires to be, beneath our continuing desire to write an imaginative new chapter in our smokestack biography, and make no mistake, that's saying something for a wee lad fae Townhead.

see the ten – pages 35-44
the mac
mackintosh house
willow tea rooms
ruchill church hall
queens cross church
martyrs' public school
the lighthouse
house for an art lover
daily record building
scotland street school

top-ten-glasgow-guide.com
facebook.com/toptenglasgowguide
twitter.com/toptenglasgow

WEE GLESGA
A POCKET GUIDE TO GLASGOW

burrell collection and pollok park

lowdown

He may not have had pockets as deep as Getty or Hearst, but Sir William Burrell (1861-1958) definitely knew his stuff when it came to collectors' items.

He's universally considered as having been years ahead of his time, having belied his shy, conservative demeanour & pioneered almost single-handedly the innovative trend of heavily researching & recovering extremely indiscrete Kangxi wares, Han and Tang burial figures, magical artefacts from the Song and Ming dynasties, remnants from the Bronze Age and much, much more.

Burrell had an eye on the preservation of what he'd amassed when he commanded that if the City wanted to show it all off, it'd have to be done in a building well away from the pollution of the City Centre (which at that time was completely smog-ridden from the shipyards). It took some time therefore, but we finally managed to find a pocket of finely-aired excellence in what is now known as (and

has won awards for being) the best park in Europe, Pollok Country Park.

contact
Tel: +44 141 287 2550
Email:
museums@glasgowlife.org.uk

social
glasgowlife.org.uk
facebook.com/theburrellcolle
ction.glasgowmuseums

when
10am-midnight Mon-Thu & Sat
11am-5pm Fri & Sun

where
Pollok Country Park
Pollokshaws Road
Glasgow, G43 1AT

top-ten-glasgow-guide.com
facebook.com/toptenglasgowguide
twitter.com/toptenglasgow

glasgow cathedral precinct

lowdown

Here's where Glasgow was born in the 6th century. Take a walk around our oldest manse, the Provand's Lordship, cross the street to the St. Mungo Museum, then head inside to our oldest building, Glasgow Cathedral, and the austere Necropolis cemetery.

You can also spend time around the area and have a look at the awesome structure of the Glasgow Royal Infirmary hospital, the Barony Church on the High Street (where I graduated from university, wet behind the ears!), the Barony North Glasgow Evangelical Church on Cathedral Square, or the historical delights of Townhead where my Dad grew up, including Martyrs School in Parson Street which was designed by a young Charles Rennie Mackintosh, and also St. Mungo's Church again on Parson Street.

Might sound like just a few good looking buildings, but type "Glasgow sectarianism" into the search engines & you might learn of their significance in our gloriously torrid history!

take a gander with st. mungo

glasgowlife.org.uk

top-ten-glasgow-guide.com
facebook.com/toptenglasgowguide
twitter.com/toptenglasgow

WEE GLESCA
A POCKET GUIDE TO GLASGOW

botanic gardens and kibble palace

lowdown

It could be Bard in the Botanics, Scotland's biggest & best-loved festival of Shakespeare that's held annually within the grounds. There's the "A" listed 19th century iron and glasshouse mastery of Kibble Palace, with its world renowned collection of temperate plants that stem (oh boy!) back over hundreds of years, its sought-after collection of statues including Scipioni Tandolini's outstanding 19th century statue of Eve which forms the centrepiece of the collection, as well as its magically hidden orchestral chamber under one of its ponds. Or it could just as very well be the grass upon which to lay your back! Whatever it is that makes hundreds of thousands of visitors spend time here I reckon you might want to find out for yourself.

The heritage trail around the gardens can take you around an hour and a half, and on the trail you'll come across North Park House which Isabella Elder, wife of John Elder who founded the Fairfield Shipyard in Govan, converted into one of the UK's first arts and medicine colleges for women; you'll be able to meander through the impressive World Rose Garden and its 9/11 Fireman's Memorial Tree, which was dedicated by the union members of the Scottish Region fire brigade; and you'll also see the ruins of the North Woodside Flint Mill which, amongst other things, was used to grind gunpowder during the Napoleonic wars.

contact
Tel: +44 141 276 1614
Email:
glasgowbotanicgardens.com/
contact

social
glasgowbotanicgardens.com/
facebook.com/GlasgowBotani
cGardens
twitter.com/GlasgowBotanic

when
Usually about 10am to dusk, check website for details.

where
730 Great Western Road
Glasgow, G12 0UE

top-ten-glasgow-guide.com
facebook.com/toptenglasgowguide
twitter.com/toptenglasgow

WEE GLESGA
A POCKET GUIDE TO GLASGOW

glasgow university

lowdown

Potted history of the uni: Established in the grounds of Glasgow Cathedral in 1451 by papal bull of Pope Nicholas V. Fourth oldest university in English-speaking world. Nexus of the Scottish Enlightenment. Pioneered higher education beyond upper classes and between the sexes. Moved to Gilmorehill in 1870 following Industrial Revolution. Seen through its doors the likes of Prime Ministers Sir Henry Campbell-Bannerman & Andrew Bonar Law, absolute zero scientist Lord Kelvin, 'father of economics' Adam Smith, steam engine innovator James Watt, TV addict John Logie Baird, world's most respected empiricist & inspiration to Immanuel Kant David Hume, the founding First Minister of Scotland Donald Dewar, a venerable clutch of Nobel laureates, and my mate Alan Macdonald.

The architecture itself is stunning to experience. You can visit the Hunterian, Mackintosh House, University Chapel and capture some of the most awe-inspiring photos you might ever get the chance to take.

contact

Tel: +44 141 330 2000
Email:
gla.ac.uk/about/contact/

social

gla.ac.uk/
facebook.com/glasgowuniversity
twitter.com/glasgowuni

when

Varies throughout the year, check website for details.

where

(main campus)
University Avenue
Glasgow, G12 8QQ

riverside transport museum

lowdown
There's not many cities who can boast as much as Glasgow a heritage and track record of innovation in world transport & technology. The Riverside Museum of Transport and Travel captures this in great detail, housing within its awe-inspiring architecture over 3,000 exhibits that you can interact with and learn about.

You can climb aboard ancient locomotive trams, subway cars, train carriages, buses and more, taking you through the ages and confirming for you just how easy it is to take modern transport for granted.

My favourite part of the museum is the old street recreated from 1895 to 1930 that you can meander down, popping in and out of an Edwardian photography studio, a 1930's Italian Café, a 1960's garage, and of course an ol' Glesca pub.

With exhibits floating above your head, and interactive display screens throughout, you'll find it hard to tear yourself away & head out to our dear "Tall Ship", the Glenlee, but make sure you don't miss it; built in this City it went on to circumnavigate the globe 4 times & survive Cape Horn 15 times, and is one of the few core historic UK vessels reflecting the mastery of Clydebuilt technology.

contact
Tel: +44 141 287 2720
Email:
museums@glasgowlife.org.uk

social
glasgowlife.org.uk
facebook.com/riverside.glasgowmuseums
twitter.com/riversidemuseum

when
10am-5pm Mon-Thu & Sat
11am-5pm Fri & Sun

where
100 Pointhouse Place
Glasgow
G3 8RS

WEE GLESGA
-•-
A POCKET GUIDE TO GLASGOW
-•-

gallery of modern art

lowdown

GoMA lives in the house of a tobacco lord from the 18th century, but don't let that put you off!

It might be more famous for the iconic image outside of Marochetti's statue of the Duke of Wellington, adorned proudly by students with a traffic cone on his head, but GoMA is *so* much more than that.

It's Scotland's most visited modern art gallery, is entirely free, and hosts a rotation of some of the world's most sought after, thought-provoking exhibitions.

I like to pop in whenever I'm nearby, as the exhibitions, workshops, performances and extensive library of art history & design evolve continuously, so there's always something new to see, particularly during the outstanding Glasgow International Festival of Visual Art every year.

And don't worry about the throng of goths & emos usually hanging around outside, with their sub-cultural darkness & skateboarding antics – they're harmless, and in my mind the fact they find comfort here just reflects how contemporary & unique the place is.

contact

Tel: +44 141 287 3050
Email:
museums@glasgowlife.org.uk

social

glasgowlife.org.uk
facebook.com/galleryofmoder
nart.glasgowmuseums
twitter.com/glasgowgoma

when

10am-5pm Mon-Wed & Sat
10am-8pm Thu
11am-5pm Fri & Sun

where

Royal Exchange Square
Glasgow
G1 3AH

glasgow science centre (+IMAX)

lowdown

Science centres have been popping up in a great many cities in recent years. We got ours in 2001, and since then it's been working on its long-term vision of promoting science and technology through thought provoking, fun, exciting, interactive experiences that inspire all to explore and understand the world around us.

There's an absolutely huge interactive science hall, Scotland's biggest IMAX cinema and best planetarium, Glasgow Tower (which, when it works (!) is the world's only fully rotating building), and superb exhibits and shows throughout the year.

It's just an absolutely inspirational way to spend a day, with kids or without, so make sure you head along and expand your mind, and if you manage to get up the tower on a day it's operational, send me the photos!

contact

Tel: +44 141 420 5000
Email:
glasgowsciencecentre.org/contact-us.html

social

glasgowsciencecentre.org/
facebook.com/Glasgowsciencecentre
twitter.com/gsc1

when

10am-5pm Mon-Sun
10am-5pm Wed-Sun (winter)
IMAX times vary per film & event

where

50 Pacific Quay
Glasgow
G51 1EA

top-ten-glasgow-guide.com
facebook.com/toptenglasgowguide
twitter.com/toptenglasgow

WEE GLESCA
A POCKET GUIDE TO GLASGOW

peoples palace and winter gardens

lowdown

This is the place you can learn more about our social history from the 18th Century and onwards, the story of the people of Glasgow. In the myriad of photos, paintings, artefacts, and interactive displays, you can experience what it was like to live here through the ages.

We're often lauded as amongst the most friendly folks on the planet, which could be explained partly as the result of generations of social deprivation and inequality. Through poor health & overcrowding as the City exploded onto the world stage, with the influx of the Irish over time and horrible events like the Calton weavers massacre, our infamous Glesca patter developed together with our unique approach to life and all its laughable social conditioning. In this museum you'll see us through the ages at work, rest & play, at "the Steamie", the single end tenements, "doon the watter", & "at the dancin".

At the fabulous Victorian glasshouse of the Winter Gardens you can also see the world's largest terracotta fountain, the Doulton, and a vast array of tropical plants and flora.

Visiting here will wipe off some of the gloss thrust in your face by the tourist industry, and introduce you to the ordinary, working class folks who made, and still make, this industrious, light-hearted City what she is.

contact
Tel: +44 141 276 0788
Email:
museums@glasgowlife.org.uk

social
glasgowlife.org.uk
facebook.com/PeoplesPalace.GlasgowMuseums
twitter.com/PeoplesPalaceGL

when
10am-5pm Tue-Thu & Sat
11am-5pm Fri & Sun
10am-5pm daily (winter gardens)

where
Glasgow Green
Glasgow
G40 1AT

top-ten-glasgow-guide.com
facebook.com/toptenglasgowguide
twitter.com/toptenglasgow

WEE GLESCA
A POCKET GUIDE TO GLASGOW

music

top-ten-glasgow-guide.com
facebook.com/toptenglasgowguide
twitter.com/toptenglasgow

WEE GLESCA
A POCKET GUIDE TO GLASGOW

king tut's wah wah hut

lowdown

Since it opened in 1990, King Tut's has been at the forefront of the Scottish live music scene & continues to be one of the most celebrated venues in the world.

It's an integral part of Glasgow's thriving grassroots music scene as well as bringing the most exciting new talent around to the City. Playing a gig at this 300 capacity venue has become a seminal point in the career of an impressive array of artists leading NME to name King Tut's 'Britain's Best Small Venue' in 2011, and 'quite possibly the finest small venue in the world' in 2007. Radio 1 also named it 'UK's Best Live Venue' three years in a row and King Tut's was voted number 7 in New York Magazine's 'Follow Your Bliss List' – a list of fifty euphoria-inducing destinations to visit before you die (above climbing Mount Kilimanjaro and Swimming with Hippos in Botswana!).

King Tut's is an exciting showcase for new and emerging bands and as the venue that supported some of the music industry's biggest names at the start of their careers: from Oasis (who were famously signed by Alan McGee at the venue in 1993) to Radiohead, The Killers, Juliette Lewis, Pulp, My Chemical Romance, Florence & The Machine, Biffy Clyro, Manic Street Preachers, Snow Patrol, Frightened Rabbit and Paolo Nutini plus many, many, more in between. The venue also has its own Record Label and Lager as well as a highly acclaimed food menu.

contact
Tel: +44 141 221 5179
Buy tickets at Ticketmaster
Email:
museums@glasgowlife.org.uk

social
kingtuts.co.uk/
facebook.com/kingtutswahw
ahhut
twitter.com/kingtuts

when
11am to midnight Mon-Sat
12noon to midnight Sun

where
272a St. Vincent Street
Glasgow
G2 5RL

---

top-ten-glasgow-guide.com
facebook.com/toptenglasgowguide
twitter.com/toptenglasgow

WEE GLESCA

A POCKET GUIDE TO GLASGOW

the glasgow barrowland ballroom

lowdown

Although many consider that the O2 Academy has now surpassed it, my favourite of all the Glasgow music venues, the Barras, has been voted in the past the greatest venue in the UK, and moreover one of the top small venues in Europe.

It's got a capacity of about 1,900, and still plays host to some of the cooler, up-and-coming acts in the world, together with larger acts who are looking for a more intimate but explosive Glasgow music venue. It'll remain dear to my heart as the first place I ever crowd-surfed (for those not in the know, this is being hoisted in the air and carried on your back by the upstretched hands of the crowd until you reach the front & get sent back into the crowd by security - always make sure your wallet's safe in your pocket before trying this!) - an amazing experience everyone should try at least once! A gig at the Barras will leave you dripping in sweat but happier than Larry (and he really is pretty darn happy), so best to take something warm to wear when you get back out into the cold.

Again though, just book a ticket & go here - I've lost count of the number of times I've seen acts perform here and then at the SECC (or now the Hydro) when they become more famous, but I leave wishing that they'd played the Barras again instead because of the superior atmosphere in this place.

contact
Tel: +44 141 552 4601
Buy tickets at Tickets Scotland
Email: manager@glasgow-barrowland.com

social
glasgow-barrowland.com/
facebook.com/groups/12532
325385
twitter.com/TheBarrowlands

when
Open only for gigs, check listings on website.

where
244 Gallowgate
Glasgow
G4 0TT

top-ten-glasgow-guide.com
facebook.com/toptenglasgowguide
twitter.com/toptenglasgow

WEE GLESGA
A POCKET GUIDE TO GLASGOW

secc, the hydro, clyde auditorium

lowdown

The Scottish Exhibition & Conference Centre, or 'the SECC' for the clever people among us, is a Glasgow music venue which cannot be ignored. Despite having had a previous reputation for being so big & square, the acoustics left you feeling like you'd just entered a ghost town rather than a concert hall, nowadays with the addition of the architecturally genius Clyde Auditorium (or the Armadillo, as it's affectionately known in these here parts, with its world-class acoustics which have the tendency to make your ears hum with satisfaction) and the even more sparkly SSE Hydro which consistently pulls in the top acts on the planet, the SECC really has turned it around.

The three of these buildings together represent Scotland's premier performance venues, and putting aside the fact that they're booked out all year round with the top performers in the world, the transformation taking place all around it on the banks of the Clyde on its own makes this place worth a visit. It's a sheer pleasure for locals like me to watch the Glasgow Music Ladder shift into position - I've seen bands play in tiny Glasgow music venues like the Glasgow Garage, move up to King Tut's, become more famous and play the Barras or the O2 Academy, and graduate proudly to these joints once they've charmed a legion of screaming fans! Book early here to avoid disappointment though.

contact

Tel: +44 141 248 3000
Buy tickets at ticketSOUP
Email: info@secc.co.uk

social

secc.co.uk/
twitter.com/SECCGlasgow
thessehydro.com/default.asp
x
facebook.com/thehydro
twitter.com/TheHydro

when

Open only for gigs, check listings on website.

where

Exhibition Way
Glasgow
G3 8YW

top-ten-glasgow-guide.com
facebook.com/toptenglasgowguide
twitter.com/toptenglasgow

WEE GLESGA
A POCKET GUIDE TO GLASGOW

royal concert hall

lowdown

This is Scotland's premier music venue, and plays host to, among others, the best classical and world music you'll find in Scotland. It regularly features outstanding operatic events, and the world's most renowned orchestras such as the Vienna Philharmonic, but also Scotland's own award-winning Royal Scottish National Orchestra, and to ensure it's not classed as too snobby, even some of the bigger names in pop music and comedy.

I try to go here as much as possible, mainly to prove that I've still got some traditional cultcha (ie. culture!) left in me, but tend to leave it for Christmas when they always put on fantastic little concerts like the Christmas West End Musicals event - you'd have to be old Scrooge himself if you didn't get in the spirit after going to one of these!

contact

Tel: +44 141 353 8000
Buy tickets at main website
Email: info@glasgowlife.com

social

glasgowconcerthalls.com/
facebook.com/GlasgowRoyal
ConcertHall
twitter.com/GCHalls

when

Open only for events, check listings on website.

where

(main office)
2 Sauchiehall Street
Glasgow, G2 3NY

top-ten-glasgow-guide.com
facebook.com/toptenglasgowguide
twitter.com/toptenglasgow

WEE GLESCA
A POCKET GUIDE TO GLASGOW

the drum and monkey

lowdown

A 'must visit' for jazz lovers out there. To be perfectly honest, I've been a few times but as I'm not a great jazz fan, it's not my cup of tea, although I'm led to believe from those more in the know than myself that this joint is the place to go for the best jazz in Glasgow. Best time to visit is on a Sunday afternoon to the evening, as sessions are held at that time every week.

I also know that other notable jazz Glasgow music venues are the Old Fruitmarket and St. Andrew's in the Square, both of which are in the Merchant City. Apologies in advance though - because of the nationwide smoking ban in public places, no longer can you languish in a smoky hovel of solitude as I'm led to believe most jazz lovers prefer!

contact

Tel: +44 141 221 6636

social

nicholsonspubs.co.uk/
twitter.com/drum_glasgow

when

11am-midnight Mon-Sat
12.30pm-11pm Sun

where

91-93 St. Vincent Street
Glasgow
G2 5TF

top-ten-glasgow-guide.com
facebook.com/toptenglasgowguide
twitter.com/toptenglasgow

WEE GLESGA
A POCKET GUIDE TO GLASGOW

13ᵗʰ note cafe

lowdown

Whatever you do, just call it 'The Note' - you'll be seen as less of a tourist if you do! This place has given me plenty of treasure trove memories over the years. It's classed as a major player in the alternative Glasgow music scene, opening its doors every night to indy, rock & blues revellers (although I'm pretty sure I've seen a folk band from Finland play there before!), hoping to catch a glimpse of something new, something kitsch. Usually, we're not disappointed.

It has been known to smell a bit like feet on occasion, but don't let that and the scarily red walls put you off - this is a tiny giant (check the oxymoron in the back!) in the Glasgow music scene, and if you're in that neck of the woods you should head there at least once when you're here.

contact

Tel: +44 141 553 1638
Email: office@13thnote.co.uk
Tel: +44 141 553 1800 (bookings)
Email:
bookings@13thnote.co.uk

social

13thnote.co.uk/
facebook.com/official13thnote
twitter.com/official13thnot

when

12noon-midnight daily
Bar & Food times vary, check site

where

50-60 King Street
Glasgow
G1 5QT

top-ten-glasgow-guide.com
facebook.com/toptenglasgowguide
twitter.com/toptenglasgow

WEE GLESGA
A POCKET GUIDE TO GLASGOW

o2 academy

lowdown

A lot of folks trendier and hipper than my old bones suggest that this is THE rung on the ladder the best bands & artists want to step onto before they really hit the big time.

I've been going to this place since it was the old Carling Academy, and have seen some absolute stunning gigs there. I've had my ears ring for weeks after an absorbing gig by The Script which left the band open-mouthed and on their knees at the thunderous appreciation they got, but I've also sat in awed silence listening to every enthralling note played by Joe Bonamassa there as he continued his journey carving out his name in blues history.

Ben Folds Five, Smashing Pumpkins, The Killers, the list goes on. And the 2,500 capacity venue which used to be a cinema back in the day also hosts comedy gigs during the Glasgow Comedy Festival.

contact

Tel: +44 141 418 3000
Box Office: 0844 477 2000
Email:
mail@o2academyglasgow.co.uk

social

o2academyglasgow.co.uk/
facebook.com/o2academygla sgow
twitter.com/O2AcademyGgow

when

Open for gigs only, check main website for listings.

where

121 Eglinton Street
Glasgow
G5 9NT

top-ten-glasgow-guide.com
facebook.com/toptenglasgowguide
twitter.com/toptenglasgow

WEE GLESGA
A POCKET GUIDE TO GLASGOW

the arches

lowdown

I remember that the List magazine once asked of this initially daunting but crazy popular Glasgow venue, how much one space could reflect the identity of an entire city? It mentioned that the Arches was the epitome of raw, slightly edgy, underground chic, and formed the creative heart of the city. A big statement, but one I readily agree with.

It may be geared up mainly for the clubbing nights, theatre, comedy & visual arts (I remember seeing here a play called Horses, Horses Coming in all Directions, which basically involved Tracey & I being watched by everyone at the start of the show, whilst a silent clown began hovering eerily around us before directing everyone in to sit underneath a huge blanket on the floor where dancers acted out a short story in the middle. Strange night that I don't think Tracey's ever forgiven me for!), but its dark, cavernous walls underneath the Central Station railway lines have also presided over some of the most electrifying & experimental live music you're ever likely to see. So it's definitely worth a pop if you can find the place!

contact

Tel: +44 141 565 1000
Email:
boxoffice@thearches.co.uk

social

thearches.co.uk/
facebook.com/TheArchesGlasgow
twitter.com/ArchesGlasgow

when

Open for gigs & events only, check main website for listings.

where

253 Argyle Street
Glasgow
G2 8DL

top-ten-glasgow-guide.com
facebook.com/toptenglasgowguide
twitter.com/toptenglasgow

WEE GLESGA
A POCKET GUIDE TO GLASGOW

nice n sleazy

lowdown

Nice 'n' Sleazy's created a template years ago for the standard Glasgow student pub & gig venue, and since then there's been a plethora of City Centre bars & Glasgow music venues which have simply copied the format with a change of name. Whilst its jukebox is internationally famous, it's known more for the live music it presents on a weekly basis.

The open-mic nights sometimes do tend to draw acts you'd prefer never to hear again, but in the main, it's a great little venue to relax, dress down and think you're cool in for a while. The main plus point? - The floors are no longer sticky since they did the place up, so if the music's making your ears bleed, you won't now be glued where you're standing and you'll be free to go upstairs for a liberating drink!

contact

Tel: +44 141 333 0900
Email: info@nicensleazy.com

social

nicensleazy.com/
facebook.com/pages/NICE-
N-SLEAZY/372060263375
twitter.com/nice_n_sleazy

when

12noon-3am Mon-Sat
1pm-3am Sun

where

421 Sauchiehall Street
Glasgow
G2 3LG

WEE GLESCA

A POCKET GUIDE TO GLASGOW

jinty mcguinty's

lowdown
I just had to mention it, because I love everything Irish! There are loads of other Irish bars dotted around Glasgow, but if you're looking for the most traditional and quality Irish Glasgow music venues, Jinty McGuinty's in Ashton Lane (just off of Byres Road in the West End) is the place you'll find your stool.

Might be a little hard to squeeze your way through the packed throng for your Guinness, but once the music gets going and the bodhran starts pounding, you'll feel like you're in Galway itself. Sláinte!

It has a superb outdoor beer garden for when it's not raining, and is a brilliant place to enjoy yourself in the cobbled street of Ashton Lane.

contact
Tel: +44 141 339 0747
Email: jinty1@hotmail.com

social
jintys.com/
facebook.com/JintyMcguinty
sIrishBar?rf=2865928880521
38
twitter.com/jintyMcGuintys

when
11am-midnight Mon-Sat
12.30pm-midnight Sun

where
23 Ashton Lane
Glasgow
G12 8SJ

WEE GLESCA
A POCKET GUIDE TO GLASGOW

cinemas

top-ten-glasgow-guide.com
facebook.com/toptenglasgowguide
twitter.com/toptenglasgow

WEE GLESCA
A POCKET GUIDE TO GLASGOW

cineworld renfrew street

lowdown
Until the new Cineworld opens at Silverburn shopping centre, this is the one Tracey and I go to most regularly.

We have a Cineworld Unlimited card which, for about £16 per month gets us unlimited movies and a fair bit off our food, as well as access to some decent premieres and advance showings.

It's the tallest cinema in Europe, has 18 screens, and is in the best location in town if you'll be in the City Centre and thinking of heading to the movies.

If you fancy an ever better experience and 3D doesn't do it for you, get one of the D-Box seats which will vibrate & shoogle you around until your teeth fall out!

contact
Tel: +44 871 200 2000
Email:
cineworld.co.uk/contact

social
cineworld.co.uk/cinemas/glasgow-renfrew-street
facebook.com/
twitter.com/cineworld

when
Open Mon-Sun, check main site for listings

where
7 Renfrew Street
Glasgow
G2 3AB

top-ten-glasgow-guide.com
facebook.com/toptenglasgowguide
twitter.com/toptenglasgow

WEE GLESCA
A POCKET GUIDE TO GLASGOW

grosvenor

lowdown

An entirely different experience from your usual cinemas here, the Grosvenor is pretty special.

It has the cosy cool atmosphere of the G.F.T. (see below), but with its comfier sofa-like seats and being licensed for alcohol, you can sit back chilled out with a beer in your hand like you're at home watching Netflix!

I go here as much as I can to see their special packaged events which they're really good at organising, for example when the Sideways movie was showing they tied it in with a wine tasting night, and I remember watching an enlightening beamback of the Hawking documentary followed by an interview and panel session with the great man himself as well as the other 'cast'.

Head to the cafe before it as there's always a tried & trusted menu available, and after the movie head up the cobbled Ashton Lane for a few drinks at the likes of Jinty's, The Chip, Vodka Wodka or Brel.

contact

Tel: +44 845 166 6002
Email:
grosvenorcinema.co.uk/contact

social

grosvenorcinema.co.uk/
facebook.com/grosvenorcinema
twitter.com/grosvenorcinema

when

Open Mon-Sun, check main site for listings

where

24 Ashton Lane
Glasgow
G12 8SJ

WEE GLESGA

A POCKET GUIDE TO GLASGOW

odeon at the quay

lowdown
My old favourite was the Odeon at Renfield Street in the centre of town, but despite its illustrious history including hosting the Beatles when they came to town, regretfully it closed.

I still love the Odeon, though, and despite its location across the bridge at the Quay, any time I'm at the bowling or visiting the Panda (one of my top restaurants in the City – see above), I'll make sure to head here to catch a flick.

It has 12 screens with state of the art audio & visual facilities, so if you're finding it difficult to get a ticket at the time you want for one of the top movies showing at Cineworld, try here instead as it ain't too far away (and vice-versa, just in case you think I'm biased towards Cineworld!).

contact
Tel: +44 871 224 4007
Email:
odeon.co.uk/contactus/

social
odeon.co.uk/cinemas/glasgow_quay
facebook.com/ODEON
twitter.com/ODEONCinemas

when
Open Mon-Sun, check main site for listings

where
Springfield Quay
Paisley Road
Glasgow
G5 8NP

81

top-ten-glasgow-guide.com
facebook.com/toptenglasgowguide
twitter.com/toptenglasgow

WEE GLESCA
A POCKET GUIDE TO GLASGOW

odeon braehead (soar / xscape)

lowdown

Since this one opened at what used to be XScape, it's become one of the top reasons to head there. Soar is full of pump-action activity, including ice-slopes, climbing, bowling and endless rib-eating!

So when you've done all that and are looking to chill for a bit at the movies, you'll thank your stars this place is so handy.

It has 12 screens, an IMAX, and most importantly, a Ben & Jerry's! Parking is ample and free outside, and don't worry about the complex closing before your late movie's done – they'll wait for you.

Soar during the day is for families, and at night it's a local hangout for the youngins – don't let that put you off though, despite it getting noisier at night them youngins wot go there tend to be the type of youngins that keep themselves to themselves.

contact
Tel: +44 871 224 4007
Email:
odeon.co.uk/contactus/

social
odeon.co.uk/cinemas/braehead/
facebook.com/ODEON
twitter.com/ODEONCinemas

when
Open Mon-Sun, check main site for listings

where
Soar at intu Braehead
King's Inch Road
Renfrew
PA4 9XU

top-ten-glasgow-guide.com
facebook.com/toptenglasgowguide
twitter.com/toptenglasgow

WEE GLESGA

A POCKET GUIDE TO GLASGOW

glasgow film theatre

lowdown

This is the focal point for the Glasgow Film Festival, the fastest growing film event in the UK, as well as the Glasgow Youth Festival, Short Film Festival, and Cinema City.

Visit their website for all the details on these, as they're becoming more popular every year thanks to the hard work of this amazing not-for-profit bunch of folks.

Having been at Rose Street for over seven decades it's well and truly the art-deco home of Glasgow cinema, and its independent roots continue to bear fruit around the City with its continuing efforts to promote the local industry & the community's knowledge of films other than the blockbusters of the day.

It recently grew a new screen, consistently pulls in more than double the UK screen average of viewers, shows films from over thirty countries around the world, and with its success continues to expand and improve its facilities.

Joss Whedon's Much Ado About Nothing, with Joss himself at the G.F.T. providing an introduction. Nuff said!

contact

Tel: +44 141 332 6535
Email:
boxoffice@glasgowfilm.org

social

glasgowfilm.org/theatre
facebook.com/glasgowfilm
twitter.com/glasgowfilm

when

Open Mon-Sun, check main site for listings

where

12 Rose Street
Glasgow
G3 6RB

top-ten-glasgow-guide.com
facebook.com/toptenglasgowguide
twitter.com/toptenglasgow

WEE GLESCA
A POCKET GUIDE TO GLASGOW

glasgow science centre imax

lowdown

Taken over by Cineworld (boys do they love Glasgow!), the science centre IMAX screen is an absolute must for goggle-eyed film fans.

If you haven't experienced the IMAX before, gie it laldy here. As it's part of the science centre they're always showing fascinating educational films on space, under the sea, the Arctic, the jungle and more, as well as the huge blockbusters of the day.

Watching a movie like this at the IMAX is mind-bending, and on more than one occasion I've grabbed hold of my seat as my brain gets fooled into thinking I'm part of the action. Talk about immersed in the moment!

It was the first IMAX in the country, has the biggest screen in Scotland (a spectacular 25m x 18.9m) and the best sound system. Located next to the Science Centre Mall, viewed widely as the best science centre in Europe, and the amazing Glasgow Tower which is the world's only fully rotational building, spending some time at Pacific Quay will be one you'll never forget!

contact

Tel: +44 141 420 5000
Email:
call.centre@glasgowsciencecentre.org

social

glasgowsciencecentre.org/imax/
facebook.com/Glasgowsciencecentre
twitter.com/gsc1

when

Open Mon-Sun, check main site for listings

where

50 Pacific Quay
Glasgow
G51 1EA

WEE GLESCA
A POCKET GUIDE TO GLASGOW

vue at glasgow fort

lowdown
This one's just outside town at the Fort shopping complex, so is a brilliant way to relax after a hard-day's retailing.

Vue cinemas are always pretty futuristic. This one's an eight screen multiplex with 3D and is the only cinema in Scotland with Dolby Atmos, a lifelike sensory experience dynamic shift in audio that's said to have reinvented traditional surround sound. The digital screens have four times the megapixels of 2k and HD, and are amongst, and may even be THE most, advanced cinema screens in the country.

The recently expanded Fort has added the Vue, a TGI Friday's, Harvester, Chiquito, Prezzo, and Pizza Express, so with the numerous places to sit yer bahooky down and eat or drink at the Fort, you could easily spend the day there.

Again, free parking and the facilities are second to none.

contact
Tel: +44 8712 240 240
Email: myvue.com/FAQs

social
myvue.com/home/cinema/glasgow-fort
facebook.com/VueCinemas
twitter.com/vuecinemas

when
Open Mon-Sun, check main site for listings

where
Glasgow Fort Shopping Park
Junction 10, M8
Glasgow
G34 9DL

top-ten-glasgow-guide.com
facebook.com/toptenglasgowguide
twitter.com/toptenglasgow

WEE GLESGA
A POCKET GUIDE TO GLASGOW

cineworld parkhead forge

lowdown

Yes another foray into Glasgow for Cineworld, it does make you think whether the company's trying to invade us! At this rate there'll be more Cineworld employees in the City than people...

In any event, it does mean that wherever you go in the City you'll never miss a film. If it's sold out in one place, try another along the road. The cinema at Parkhead is always a favourite for those shopping at the Forge or the market there, or as a precursor for those heading along to Celtic Park for the football.

Seven excellent screens, free parking, great transport links to and from the City Centre, once again Cineworld has delivered with this place. Another thing I forgot to mention in the others is that Cineworld are really big on showing not only independent & foreign movies, but also live theatre and ballet shows & concerts as well, so you'll always have

a great amount of choice when you visit and aren't sure what to feast your eyes on.

contact
Tel: 44 871 200 2000
Email:
cineworld.co.uk/contact

social
cineworld.co.uk/cinemas/glasgow-parkhead
facebook.com/cineworld
twitter.com/cineworld

when
Open Mon-Sun, check main site for listings

where
Forge Shopping Centre
1221 Gallowgate
Glasgow
G31 4EB

top-ten-glasgow-guide.com
facebook.com/toptenglasgowguide
twitter.com/toptenglasgow

WEE GLESGA

A POCKET GUIDE TO GLASGOW

cineworld silverburn

lowdown

I've included this for those planning on visiting in 2015, as this is when the fourteen-screen, 50k feet, multiplex opens at the edge of this monolith of a shopping complex at Silverburn.

The development taking shape around it at the moment will include nine new restaurants (some of which have opened already including TGI Friday's, the amazing Cosmo World Buffet & Five Guys), a Gala Bingo, additional retail and an upgraded 'public realm', whatever that is!

Once it opens, Silverburn will be absolutely gigantic, and an un-missable experience for those wanting to explore the southside of the City. Take in some culture at the Burrell Collection, breathe in the fresh air around the award-winning Pollok Park, then roll the sleeves up and spend all your hard-earned green at Silverburn.

I'll let you know once it's open, as you can be sure it'll match the usual quality of Cineworld. And I'm not just saying that as I've been brain-washed by our new Cineworld Overlords!

contact
Tel: 44 871 200 2000
Email:
cineworld.co.uk/contact

social
facebook.com/cineworld
twitter.com/cineworld

when
Open Mon-Sun, check main site for listings

where
Silverburn Shopping Centre
Barrhead Road
Glasgow
G53 6QR

top-ten-glasgow-guide.com
facebook.com/toptenglasgowguide
twitter.com/toptenglasgow

WEE GLESGA
A POCKET GUIDE TO GLASGOW

centre for contemporary arts (cca)

lowdown

A seriously cool place! Within Alexander Thomson's Grade A Grecian Chambers lurks one of the main hubs of Glasgow's world famous creative activity.

Other than the brilliant Saramago café bar that I'm prone to frequenting (and not just to convince folks that I'm "bohemian"!), all year you can experience from mainly new & challenging artists some of the planet's most cutting-edge films, music, exhibitions, literature, talks, and festivals. It's gained a reputation as a world class venue for improvised, experimental & electronic music, and plays host each year to various up & coming composers and orchestras.

The place developed from the infamous Third Eye Centre in the 1970s which was described as a "shrine to the *avant garde*" and became the centre for Glasgow counter culture, and since it became the CCA in 1992 its open source curatorial policy that's allowed artists & organisations to propose their own programmes in conjunction with those the CCA's curated, has continued to cement its place on the global stage.

So if you've a need to be inspired and fancy something different, something you won't experience elsewhere, this is definitely where you should spend some time.

contact

Tel: +44 141 352 4900
Email: gen@cca-glasgow.com

social

cca-glasgow.com
facebook.com/cca.glasgow.1
twitter.com/cca_glasgow

when

10am-midnight Mon-Sat
11am-6pm   Tue-Sat
(Galleries)

where

350 Sauchiehall Street
Glasgow
G2 3JD

WEE GLESGA

A POCKET GUIDE TO GLASGOW

shopping

top-ten-glasgow-guide.com
facebook.com/toptenglasgowguide
twitter.com/toptenglasgow

WEE GLESCA
A POCKET GUIDE TO GLASGOW

silverburn

lowdown

This place is a retail monolith. In the Southside of the City just along the road from Pollok Park and its wonderful Burrell Collection, Pollok's been transformed into one of the hottest shopping destinations in the UK.

It houses a number of flagship stores, pop-up shops, fancy little stalls, some sumptuous restaurants spanning a range of price bands, and a luxurious feel throughout despite its affordable ethos.

This is one of my wife Tracey's favourite places to shop for presents, as there's a huge range to choose from. It's also in the middle of expansion at the moment, with a huge Cineworld spawning out of the old bingo hall, more shops, a further nine restaurants including the amazing Five Guys, and, well, a new bingo hall! You could actually spend an entire day here and not get around everything, so that might give you an idea about how packed it is.

With an annual footfall of over 14 million people and at 100% occupancy, Silverburn is nothing short of retail royalty!

contact

Tel: +44 141 880 3200
Email:
enquiries@shopsilverburn.com

social

shopsilverburn.com
facebook.com/shopsilverburn
twitter.com/shopsilverburn

when

10am-9pm Mon-Fri
9am-7pm Sat
10am-6pm Sun
8.30am-10pm   Mon-Fri (dining)
9am to 10pm Sat (dining)
10am to 9pm Sun (dining)

where

Barrhead Road
Glasgow
G53 6QR

intu braehead

lowdown

At over one million square feet you might want to check your footwear's comfortable before setting off to into Braehead Shopping Centre.

It has over 100 shops, restaurants, and a massive arena which plays host to some excellent bands and artists throughout the year. It also has an ice rink and curling facilities that have held the World Championships (as well as myself in my hilarious attempts at mastering the sport!).

Although it's out of the way of the City Centre, its location is really good. It's near Glasgow Airport, next to a massive Ikea, Soar (which used to be XScape) and a retail park with 10 further stores.

It's a shopping mecca that sucks millions of visitors a year through its doors, so if you're looking for something to spend your cash on, I reckon you'll find it pretty easily here.

contact

Tel: +44 141 885 4600
Email:
braehead.information@intu.co.uk

social

intu.co.uk/braehead
facebook.com/intuBraehead
twitter.com/intuBraehead

when

10am-9pm Mon-Fri
9am-6.30pm Sat
10am-6pm Sun
Dining times vary, check site for details

where

King's Inch Road
Glasgow
G51 4BN

top-ten-glasgow-guide.com
facebook.com/toptenglasgowguide
twitter.com/toptenglasgow

WEE GLESCA

A POCKET GUIDE TO GLASGOW

glasgow fort retail park

lowdown

This is the only uncovered shopping centre in Glasgow. You might think with the weather we have, that would put this place out the picture for the citizens of Glasgow.

You'd be wrong if you did think that though, as since it opened in 2004 it's become one of the saviours of the East End of the City, with so many folks flocking there year in year out that they've now expanded it by adding a state of the art cinema, more restaurants and shops.

Coming here is a really nice experience and different from feeling cooped up indoors, and particularly at Christmas when you're walking around in the cold, hot chocolate in hand with festive music filtering through from the outdoor sound system, it makes less painful the thought that you've still not bought all your presents!

It has a great many of the big name stores as well as a few wee gems, and with 1900 parking spaces with more to come in the expansion taking place, if you're swithering about whether to come here it'll prove to be less hassle & more rewarding than you think. I speak from experience, as with so many retail centres nearer our house we still head to the Fort regularly, so that must tell you something!

contact
Tel: +44 141 771 7777
Email:
glasgowfort.com/contact

social
glasgowfort.com
facebook.com/glasgowfort
twitter.com/glasgowfort

when
10am-10pm Mon-Fri
9am-7pm Sat
10am-6pm Sun
Dining times vary, check site for details

where
Provan Walk
Junction 10, M8
Glasgow
G34 9DL

the style mile

lowdown
It annoys me sometimes when city marketing companies come up with a rebranding to attract more visitors, but hey, look at me embracing it with both arms! We used to have the 'golden z' which ran from Argyle Street, up Buchanan Street and along Sauchiehall Street. Now we have a 'style mile' block which pretty much covers the City Centre.

To be fair, there's good reason to be proud enough of the place to rebrand it, as it's mainly because of this area that Glasgow still has the mantle of being the biggest retail powerhouse in the UK after London.

From the trendy shops & craft fairs of the Merchant City, to the flagship masterpieces in the centre, and the magnificent St. Enoch Centre and Buchanan Galleries (two of the largest retail centres in the UK), you won't get round it all in a day.

There's just so much to cram in that I couldn't fit it here, so visit the links and cherry pick your top destinations before you go so that you make the most of your time here.

And pack your wallets and purses people, they're in for some action!

contact
Visit the main site for all contact details of shops & centres within the mile.

social
glasgowstylemile.com
facebook.com/PeopleMakeGl asgow
twitter.com/PeopleMakeGLA

when
Visit the main site for details of each area and shops within the mile.

where
Right in the city centre & Merchant City, ye cannae miss it!

top-ten-glasgow-guide.com
facebook.com/toptenglasgowguide
twitter.com/toptenglasgow

WEE GLESCA
A POCKET GUIDE TO GLASGOW

the west end

lowdown

There are a few big stores in the West End, but mainly this is where you want to go for the hipper, trendier, funkier, studenty independent shopping experience.

A lot of the stores you'll find are run by families & friends, selling crafts, fiddly things, unique furniture and clothing, souvenirs you won't find anywhere else. Down the magnificently understated cobbled Cresswell Lane, along Ruthven Lane where you'll find second hand goods aplenty as well as some hidden restaurants you'll be talking about for years, and in and around the other wee lanes and streets meandering through the area, you'll find that it's a far more relaxing, less commercial and inspirational way to shop.

There's a whole lotta arty cool in this neck of the woods, and you'll want to come back for more when you get the chance.

contact

Visit Pat's site below for all contact details of shops within the West End.

social

glasgowwestend.co.uk
facebook.com/pages/Pats-Guide-to-Glasgows-West-End
twitter.com/glasgowswestend

when

Visit Pat's site above for details of each area and shops within the West End.

where

Err, find the city centre, head west! Plenty of public transport links available only a few minutes ride.

top-ten-glasgow-guide.com
facebook.com/toptenglasgowguide
twitter.com/toptenglasgow

WEE GLESGA

A POCKET GUIDE TO GLASGOW

markets

lowdown

Despite the ever absorbing consumerism stretching across Glasgow over the years, she's never lost her love for markets.

From the world-famous Barras, to the tourists' favourite Sloans Market which operates beside Sloans (the 18th Century masterpiece and Glasgow's oldest bar & restaurant), to the trendy craft fairs in Merchant Square, to the second-hand life saviour of the Jack & Jill Markets that cater for parents looking for a bargain, to the joyful Christmas Markets in the City Centre, and to the traditional 'we have it all' market at the Forge, you'll have choice in abundance and never have the excuse that you couldn't find what you were looking for.

Going to a market is a totally different experience, and for me way more satisfying, because you always get the feeling that you know where your money's going and that what you're buying will have been hand-crafted or created lovingly by people passionate about making a living from their own hands & ingenuity.

Have a look at some of the links here to get a flavour of the best markets in town. Watch out for the car boot sales around the city as well, as they're always another great way to grab a deal.

contact

Visit each site here for more details.

social

sloansglasgow.com/market
glasgow-barrowland.com/
merchantcityglasgow.com/event/merchant-square-craft-design-fair/
glasgowloveschristmas.com/
forgemarket.co.uk
jackandjillmarket.co.uk

when

Visit each site here for more details.

where

Visit each site here for more details.

top-ten-glasgow-guide.com
facebook.com/toptenglasgowguide
twitter.com/toptenglasgow

WEE GLESCA
A POCKET GUIDE TO GLASGOW

parkhead forge

lowdown

The Forge Shopping Centre is named after the old Beardmore steel works which was the biggest employer in the area but sadly closed in 1976, borne from the massive regeneration project which followed the closure. You might think that it's just a shopping centre, but its roots are set squarely in helping the local community and we support it as much as we can.

Point of local knowledge: the reason the centre's formed with big glass triangles is testament to the Beardmore Glacier, one of the world's largest valley glaciers in Antarctica, named after Sir William Beardmore who owned the steel works & funded Ernest Shackleton's expedition to the Antarctic in 1908.

There's a retail park, cinema and huge market surrounding it, and it's becoming an even more popular place to visit for the reinvigorated East End of the City following the Commonwealth Games.

The centre's continually working to employ and engage the local community with its various projects, and aside from all that it's just a superb place to splash the cash!

contact

Tel: +44 141 556 6661
Email: customerservices@forgeshopping.com

social

forgeshopping.com
facebook.com/ForgeParkhead
twitter.com/forgeShopping

when

8.30am-8pm Mon Wed
8.30pm-9pm Thu & Fri
8am-8pm Sat
9am-6pm Sun

where

1221 Gallowgate
Glasgow
G31 4EB

top-ten-glasgow-guide.com
facebook.com/toptenglasgowguide
twitter.com/toptenglasgow

WEE GLESCA
A POCKET GUIDE TO GLASGOW

independent music stores

lowdown

Glasgow is a UNESCO City of Music, plays host to an average of 130 shows each week more than any other Scottish city, and has a deep history in music that spans every style.

As with everywhere else, despite this rich love of all things musical our historical fascination with the music store has diminished over time, in favour of the dreaded download & cheap bargains at the supermarket.

Still raging against the machine, the record store ain't finished yet! Check the links here to the brave independent souls who still welcome hoards of customers through their doors every day. As they're absent online I'll also mention the legendary Missing Records in Argyle Street, Play It Again Records in Ruthven Lane, and Record Fayre in Chisholm Street.

Vinyl's still fighting the good fight, and in these stores you'll also find selections & records of music across all genres that you'd be hard pressed to find beyond the highlighted barriers of the download charts.

I may sound old and past it, but the days of spending hours with your mates flicking through the racks until finding that one mysterious unknown record that'll change your life forever, will simply never be topped by mouse-scrolling & being told what to listen to by programmed menus.

Support your local stores people, lest there be even more soul-stripping in music.

contact

Visit the links here or if there's no links, ask me or Google it.

social

twitter.com/Monorail_Music
twitter.com/rubadub_glasgow
twitter.com/LoveMusicGlasgo
twitter.com/mixeduprecords
twitter.com/volcanictongue
twitter.com/FoppByresRoad

when

Visit the links here or if there's no links, ask me or Google it.

where

Visit the links here or if there's no links, ask me or Google it.

top-ten-glasgow-guide.com
facebook.com/toptenglasgowguide
twitter.com/toptenglasgow

WEE GLESCA
A POCKET GUIDE TO GLASGOW

scottish souvenir shops

lowdown

Everywhere we go on holiday I'm dragged by my wife Tracey to a souvenir shop. Strike that, *every* souvenir shop she can find!

We tend to self-deprecate here about being Scottish, so unlike in Edinburgh there ain't too many opportunities here for tourists to buy up tartan souvenirs. But don't worry, there are some brilliant places to go if that's exactly what you want, a little piece of traditional, stereotypical Scottishness!

Here I've included some links to souvenir and kilt shops in Glasgow, but also everywhere in the City Centre, Merchant City, West End & Southside there's a myriad of shops and markets stalls selling uniquely Scottish, hand-made crafts, gifts, jewellery and clothing, so make sure you take some time to browse the smaller non-chain-type shops while you're here.

If you need anything else though and can't find it, let me know and I'll see what I can do.

contact

Visit the links here or if there's no links, ask me or Google it.

social

tartanplus.co.uk
theheritageofscotland.co.uk
gilt-edged.co.uk
slanjkilts.com

when

Visit the links here or if there's no links, ask me or Google it.

where

Visit the links here or if there's no links, ask me or Google it.

top-ten-glasgow-guide.com
facebook.com/toptenglasgowguide
twitter.com/toptenglasgow

WEE GLESGA

A POCKET GUIDE TO GLASGOW

farmers' markets

lowdown

I'll never forget the Armstrong & Miller Show on TV which slagged off farmers markets, as it was a pretty hilarious send up of how they sell pretty much what you can buy in a supermarket, but at twice the price!

Despite their reputation though, I'd still recommend a visit to one of these around the City. By and large you'll get fresh cuts of all types of meat and fish, and on a number of occasions I've found that supermarkets in fact *don't* sell some of the meats the markets have. Stick that in your pipe and smoke it TV comedians!

Aside from anything else, whilst farmers do pretty well by selling to supermarkets, they don't do that well and could always do with some support from the local community to ensure the survival of farms in the area.

As much as well can we'll pop down to our local one, and pick up some amazing sausages, cheeses, preservatives and sauces to use for dinner that night. So if you're touring about here and come across a farmers market, buying something there will give you the glow of helping sustain local farming whilst giving you something of quality to chew on!

contact
Check sites for details.

social
scottishfarmersmarkets.co.uk
citypropertyglasgow.co.uk/

when
Check sites for details. Usually every 2nd Saturday morning & early afternoon.

where
Check sites for details.

top-ten-glasgow-guide.com
facebook.com/toptenglasgowguide
twitter.com/toptenglasgow

WEE GLESGA
•◆•
A POCKET GUIDE TO GLASGOW
•◆•

theatres

WEE GLESCA

A POCKET GUIDE TO GLASGOW

tramway

lowdown

This amazing building's more than just a theatre. It's an international art-space which commissions, produces & presents contemporary arts projects, to inspire and add to our understanding of today's world by connecting audiences and artists.

Tramway is a space where you're welcomed to witness, engage, experience, participate, to be challenged and to learn.

Peter Brook once said of the place that it's "an industrial cathedral that connects art with humanity. It's real, it speaks of the city's history, it speaks of Glasgow". Tramway is Scotland's internationally acclaimed venue for contemporary visual and performing art, its reputation founded upon its commitment to the presentation of the most innovative work by Scottish and international artists. The very distinctive architecture (it used to be the Coplawhill tram shed, hence its name!), character and history of the venue itself have ensured that Tramway is a unique place to produce and experience the best in contemporary art.

The huge attendance records being broken at the venue prove just how much the City's continuing to embrace cutting-edge performance, and I'd highly recommend the youth theatre productions here for that reason.

contact
Tel: +44 141 276 0950
Email: info@tramway.org

social
tramway.org/Pages/home.as px
facebook.com/GlasgowTram way
twitter.com/glasgowtramway

when
9.30am-8pm Tue-Sat
12noon-6pm Sun
12noon-5pm Tue-Fri (exhibitions)

where
25 Albert Drive
Glasgow
G41 2PE

WEE GLESGA
A POCKET GUIDE TO GLASGOW

theatre royal

lowdown

The oldest theatre in the City, the Theatre Royal opened on 28th November 1867 as the Royal Colosseum and Opera House with an interesting performance called The Laughing Hyena, and after two fires re-opened in September 1895. It's been called "the most conscious building in the City", is the longest running theatre in the country and is still associated with the best in the world of entertainment. It continues to present a wide variety of drama, dance, comedy, opera, musical and children's theatre, is home to Scotland's resident companies, Scottish Opera and Scottish Ballet, and is a unique City Centre venue for conferences, meetings and seminars.

The Victorian auditorium and stylish contemporary corporate areas provide privacy and flexibility for many occasions. I've been to a great many wonderful performances here, and following a massive revamp completed in 2014 the facilities here are second to none.

So be sure to grab a bit of entertainment history when you visit by nabbing a ticket for whatever's playing here.

contact

Tel: +44 844 871 7627
Email:
atgtickets.com/customer-care/contact-us/

social

atgtickets.com/venues/theatre-royal-glasgow/
facebook.com/kingsandtheatreroyalglasgow
twitter.com/GlasgowKings

when

Check website for listings.

where

282 Hope Street
Glasgow
G2 3QA

WEE GLESCA
A POCKET GUIDE TO GLASGOW

tron theatre

lowdown

The Tron aims to present the people of Glasgow and the West of Scotland with outstanding professional productions of the finest new writing of the last ten years, with an emphasis on world, UK and Scottish premieres.

It opened as a theatre club in 1979, rising from the ashes of the destroyed Close Theatre, based at the Citizens' Theatre mentioned below. Originally based in the Victorian bar of the Tron whilst the Kirk itself was transformed into the auditorium, the Tron has become a leading player in Scottish theatre. It's established itself as a powerhouse of both new writing and dynamic productions of classic texts, making full use of available Scottish talent.

The Tron is also an established receiving theatre on the small-middle scale, as well as a major venue for many of Glasgow's festivals including Celtic Connections, Glasgow International Jazz Festival, Glasgow International Comedy Festival, the Merchant City Festival and Glasgay!

Another major draw of the Tron, of course, is the superb bar & kitchen which I've tended to relax in even if I'm not there for a performance.

contact

Tel: +44 141 552 4267
Email: box.office@tron.co.uk

social

tron.co.uk
facebook.com/trontheatre
twitter.com/trontheatre

when

Check website for listings.

where

63 Trongate
Glasgow
G1 5HB

top-ten-glasgow-guide.com
facebook.com/toptenglasgowguide
twitter.com/toptenglasgow

WEE GLESGA
A POCKET GUIDE TO GLASGOW

kings theatre

lowdown

This is probably the theatre I've attended most in my life. Consistently it attracts the touring productions of the best of the West End & Broadway musicals, and I could count on about at least ten hands the number of breathtaking performances I've seen there.

It opened in 1904, but far more interestingly than that it plays host to one of the top pantomimes you'll experience on the planet. There's always a competition between here and the Pav for the best show, but whichever one you go for you'll be sure to have a night you'll never forget!

In 2014 I had the joy here of capturing Wicked, which shattered new attendance records for the Kings and for me was one of the top five musical productions I've ever seen. On a regular basis I'm astounded by how a venue as small as this can take a huge West End production & condense it without affecting the quality, and in fact enhance it given the more intimate feeling from the smaller theatre.

If you get the chance, therefore, book a ticket here but get in quick as it's often sold out.

contact

Tel: +44 844 871 7627
Email:
atgtickets.com/customer-care/contact-us/

social

atgtickets.com/venues/kings-theatre/
facebook.com/kingsandtheatreroyalglasgow
twitter.com/GlasgowKings

when

Check website for listings.

where

297 Bath Street
Glasgow
G2 4JN

---

top-ten-glasgow-guide.com
facebook.com/toptenglasgowguide
twitter.com/toptenglasgow

WEE GLESCA
A POCKET GUIDE TO GLASGOW

citizens theatre

lowdown

First opened as a theatre in 1878, and established as a citizens' theatre in 1945, it aims to present a mixture of contemporary versions of classic plays and new Scottish drama. It works with writers, directors and companies that have a reputation for producing outstanding work to deliver truly inspirational live theatre, and has extensive backstage workshop facilities to make its own sets and costumes, being the only theatre in Scotland still to have the original Victorian machinery under the stage and the original Victorian paint frame is still used today to paint the backcloths for shows..

Its Citizens Learning team is committed to enhancing the lives of all kinds and ages of people in Glasgow and beyond, producing theatre for children and young people, community productions and delivering a pioneering range of creative participatory projects for varied communities and in the education sector.

It's the world's oldest fully functioning professional theatre which retains the greater part of its historic auditorium and stage, but belying its age it pumps out every year some truly cutting-edge and thought-provoking productions for kids and adults alike.

Aside from anything else though, after a performance here I always leave with a feeling that I've just delved more into and supported the community around me.

contact
Tel: +44 141 429 0022
Email: citz.co.uk/enquiry

social
citz.co.uk
facebook.com/citizenstheatre
twitter.com/citizenstheatre

when
Check website for listings.

where
119 Gorbals Street
Glasgow
G5 9DS

top-ten-glasgow-guide.com
facebook.com/toptenglasgowguide
twitter.com/toptenglasgow

WEE GLESCA
A POCKET GUIDE TO GLASGOW

glasgow's concert halls

lowdown

Yup, I'm well aware I'm cheating by including three venues in one, but given that they're all run under the one umbrella organisation then it ain't just me!

The Royal Concert Hall is Scotland's premier performance venue, hosts Celtic Connections & the Royal Scottish National Orchestra, as well as over 400 concerts & 1,000 corporate events every year.

The City Halls, built in 1841 & the focus for Glasgow's Centre for Music, are the City's oldest & most loved purpose built performance and meeting space. The BBC Scottish Symphony Orchestra is housed here as is the Scottish Music Centre, and the Scottish Chamber Orchestra squeezes in as well.

The Old Fruitmarket used to be, well, an old fruit market, but is now an absolutely stunning venue that plays host to as this hugely versatile venue has already played host to theatre events, jazz concerts, comedy, rock, pop and world music gigs as well as club nights, ceilidhs, fashion shows and banquets. One thing for sure is that an amazing atmosphere is guaranteed!

OK, so they're not really theatres, but they *have* hosted theatre performances and I couldn't have completed a City performance guide like this without them, so leave me alone! ☺

contact

Tel: +44 141 353 8000
Email:
glasgowconcerthalls.com/contact-us

social

glasgowconcerthalls.com
facebook.com/GlasgowRoyal
ConcertHall
facebook.com/TheOldFruitm
arket
facebook.com/glasgowcityhal
ls
twitter.com/GCHalls

when

Check website for listings.

where

Glasgow Life
2 Sauchiehall Street
Glasgow
G2 3NY

pavilion theatre

lowdown

Ah, the Pav!

It was the first theatre in Glasgow I ever visited, or at least remember visiting, and I can still recall throwing boiled sweets and laughing uncontrollably throughout my first pantomime performance there.

It's one of the most famous stages in Scottish culture. From Mrs. Brown to Billy Connolly, Rikki Fulton, Sydney Devine and the Krankies, the Pavilion Theatre's been the breeding ground for some of the most successful stage stars in the UK.

The Pav's the only theatre in Scotland that isn't subsidised by the Scottish Arts Council yet is still packed to the gunnels every night. It's been said of the place that it's the David up against the Goliaths of the theatre world, being a tiny theatre run by a Scottish family, but is still bums-on-seats-wise one of the most successful in the UK.

It remains the last stronghold in Glasgow's long music hall tradition, but rather than coming across as a sad reflection of great days of old that have passed their sell-by date, thankfully we still hold it dear to our hearts and attend in our droves every year looking for a bit more variety in our lives!

Ah the Pav, long live the Pav!...

contact

Tel: +44 844 332 1846
Email:
sales@paviliontheatre.co.uk

social

paviliontheatre.co.uk
facebook.com/paviliontheatre
twitter.com/GlasgowPavilion

when

Check website for listings.

where

121 Renfield Street
Glasgow
G2 3AX

top-ten-glasgow-guide.com
facebook.com/toptenglasgowguide
twitter.com/toptenglasgow

WEE GLESGA
A POCKET GUIDE TO GLASGOW

the arches

lowdown

I remember that the List magazine once asked of this initially daunting but crazy popular Glasgow venue, how much one space could reflect the identity of an entire city? It mentioned that the Arches was the epitome of raw, slightly edgy, underground chic, and formed the creative heart of the city. A big statement, but one I readily agree with.

It may be geared up mainly for the clubbing nights, theatre, comedy & visual arts (I remember seeing here a play called Horses, Horses Coming in all Directions, which basically involved Tracey & I being watched by everyone at the start of the show, whilst a silent clown began hovering eerily around us before directing everyone in to sit underneath a huge blanket on the floor where dancers acted out a short story in the middle. Strange night that I don't think Tracey's ever forgiven me for!), but its dark, cavernous walls underneath the Central Station railway lines have also presided over some of the most electrifying & experimental live music you're ever likely to see. So it's definitely worth a pop if you can find the place!

contact

Tel: +44 141 565 1000
Email:
boxoffice@thearches.co.uk

social

thearches.co.uk/
facebook.com/TheArchesGlasgow
twitter.com/ArchesGlasgow

when

Open for gigs & events only, check main website for listings.

where

253 Argyle Street
Glasgow
G2 8DL

top-ten-glasgow-guide.com
facebook.com/toptenglasgowguide
twitter.com/toptenglasgow

WEE GLESGA
A POCKET GUIDE TO GLASGOW

òran mór

lowdown
This place is pretty strange. There I said it!

The reason I said it is that, well, it's pretty strange. It can entertain pretty much every generation of your family. In the whisky bar ol' granddad can sample fine malts & read the paper until his lunchtime nap; meanwhile mum & dad can relax in the beer garden ordering quality Scots fare & tipples to while away the hours until their parental duties kick back in; and later on down in the crypt, the teenage dreamers will bust moves in one of the best clubs in Glasgow.

Like I say, pretty strange. It's become famous also for its intimate & inspirational A Play, A Pie, and A Pint, which, if you've not experienced it before, is exactly what you think it is, and forms the core of festivals, private functions and meeting plans.

Spending some time here in the grand but homely surroundings will make you feel pretty laid back. And so as the name suggests, it truly is a great melody of life!

contact
Tel: +44 141 357 6200
Email: info@oran-mor.co.uk

social
oran-mor.co.uk/
facebook.com/OranMorGlasgow
twitter.com/oranmorglasgow

when
Check website for show, bar, restaurant & club opening times.

where
Top of Byres Road
Glasgow
G12 8QX

top-ten-glasgow-guide.com
facebook.com/toptenglasgowguide
twitter.com/toptenglasgow

WEE GLESGA
A POCKET GUIDE TO GLASGOW

cottier theatre

lowdown

I've included this wee place as it's one my favourite performance venues in the City.

Located in an atmospherically gothic church conversion in the West End of Glasgow it houses a theatre, bar, excellent restaurant surrounded by a garden with stone terraces for eating outside in the summer.

Given the space available it'll always be more of an intimate performance you'll come to see here, but a great many I've seen have absolutely packed a punch despite the size.

As with many other theatres in the City you'll have the opportunity of witnessing a pantomime in the festive period, but throughout the year make sure you check the programme as there are always a few hidden gems you'd otherwise miss were you to focus only on the bigger venues.

contact
Tel: +44 141 357 5825
Email: theatre@cottiers.com

social
cottiers.com
facebook.com/cottiersglasgow
twitter.com/CottiersTheatre

when
Check website for listings.

where
93-95 Hyndland Street
Glasgow
G11 5PU

WEE GLESGA

A POCKET GUIDE TO GLASGOW

hidden gem eateries

WEE GLESCA
•••
A POCKET GUIDE TO GLASGOW
•••

the hanoi bike shop

lowdown

OK, so I admit that before this place came along my knowledge of Vietnam had been formed largely by Hollywood and its glossed-up tales of US oppression.

Now, I can push past all the air-brushed history & simply delight here in what I'm told is the most authentic Vietnamese street food you'll experience in Scotland.

Ideal on a hot summer day (yeah we do have them occasionally!), I can't get enough of the stripped down calmness, the ice cold Saigon Export, and a stunning menu that I've still not got through completely.

If you can't choose what to eat here, ask the staff as they'll probably know more than you but won't patronise you about that & will politely guide you through a selection to suit your tastes & your own chilli spicy hot hot limits. Pho, banh mi, home made Dau Hu Gung tofu covered in lashings of spicy sriracha...I mean, who needs Hollywood?!!

contact

Tel: +44 141 334 7165
Email:
pho@thehanoibikeshop.co.uk

social

thehanoibikeshop.co.uk
facebook.com/TheHanoiBike Shop
twitter.com/Hanoibikeshop

when

Noon-11pm Mon-Wed
Noon-12.30am Thu-Fri
11am-12.30am Sat
11am-11pm Sun

where

8 Ruthven Lane
Glasgow
G12 9BG

the gannet

lowdown

This is one of the first but increasing number of understated genius eateries that's been helping transform Finnieston into a seriously chill place to, well, chill.

Walking into the small, darkened, stripped-down Gannet and pouring over its menu will probably not fill you with much excitement, but once its fine dishes have tickled your palate, I've absolutely no doubt your face will end up looking like a dog that's just been shown a card trick.

If you're opting for the small plates menu here (which I tend to do), try as much as you can but make sure you don't miss the Stornoway black pudding Scotch duck egg, and the confit lamb shoulder with onion puree & artichoke. Two stunning dishes I order pretty much every time! In the main menu I can't see past the slow cooked pork, potato terrine, apple, girolles & roast pork sauce, and to finish it all the lemon posset with Scottish strawberries & basil ice cream.

The menu changes frequently but I've never had a so-so meal here whatever's being cooked, and I always end up eating like a true gannet here, although yeah, that *has* got me thrown out a few times for squawking like a bird, which is pretty embarrassing...

contact
Tel: +44 141 204 2081
Email: info@thegannetgla.com

social
thegannetgla.com/index.php
facebook.com/TheGannetGla
twitter.com/thegannetgla

when
Noon-2.30pm Tue-Sat
5pm-9.45pm Tue-Sat
Noon-3pm Sun
5pm-8.45pm Sun

where
1155 Argyle Street
Glasgow
G3 8TB

top-ten-glasgow-guide.com
facebook.com/toptenglasgowguide
twitter.com/toptenglasgow

WEE GLESCA
A POCKET GUIDE TO GLASGOW

ox and finch

lowdown

This is Jon MacDonald's place. If you don't know Jon, he's former head chef to the well-travelled McLaren F1 team (hence the sheer variation on the menu), and one of the founders of Scoop & the amazing street food cartel that pops up in a myriad of places in town serving dishes of totally unpretentious genius.

So in his first restaurant nestled in the shabby-chic ex-oblivion Finnieston part of Glasgow, you won't be surprised by the array of delicately-crafted pieces of art on the menu.

Salt and pepper squid, blood orange, chilli & saffron aioli. Braised ox cheek with celeriac puree and bacon gremolata. House-cured gravadlax, horseradish, dill-pickled cucumber & pumpernickel and a cucumber vodka shot. Every time I visit here I end up cursing my gut for not expanding enough to allow room for more!

Book as early as you can to avoid sad disappointment, particularly on the weekends, as this place continues to be packed out well in advance.

It's so inspirational here I've been willing to forget that it's built in the same space my favourite Greek restaurant used to be before it closed. If you're reading this, then, I forgive you Jon MacDonald!

contact
Tel: +44 141 339 8627
Email: hello@oxandfinch.com

social
oxandfinch.com/
facebook.com/OxAndFinch
twitter.com/OxAndFinch

when
Noon-Midnight Sun-Sat

where
920 Sauchiehall Street
Glasgow
G3 7TF

crabshakk

lowdown

Dining in Crabshakk has always made me feel that I and everyone around me's gate-crashed some poor soul's tenement kitchenette. The place is *tiny*, and given that it's usually packed to the gunnels, you'll find that it gets pretty noisy, the sound of clattering pans in the nearby background adding to the sizzling atmosphere.

If it *is* too packed when you get there you'll likely be directed a few doors along to their 'Table 11' Oyster Bar opened more recently, but I still prefer the original space.

The reason it *is* so busy is that it's one of the best places to eat seafood in Scotland, all of it caught that day. Juicy oysters on ice, seared scallops, langoustines, crabs, lobster, fruits de mer, home cured gravadlax...sounds basic but you'll be hard pressed to find elsewhere the same level of quality & love in how it's cooked. The specials board changes regularly though, laying out more complex creations than what's offered in the main menu.

Crabshakk's been serving out amazing seafood in Finnieston since 2009, but has gained even more popularity as the area surrounding it has been regenerated. Superb way to fill your belly before walking down to the Hydro or spending a chilled-out night in the nearby bars.

contact
Tel: +44 141 334 6127
Email: info@crabshakk.com

social
crabshakk.com/restaurant/
facebook.com/pages/Crabshakk/148503655190228
twitter.com/crabshakk

when
Noon-Midnight Tue-Sun

where
1114 Argyle Street
Glasgow
G3 8TD

top-ten-glasgow-guide.com
facebook.com/toptenglasgowguide
twitter.com/toptenglasgow

WEE GLESGA
A POCKET GUIDE TO GLASGOW

buddy's, bread meats bread, ketchup

lowdown

Ok so this is another cheat's page, containing as it does at least three restaurants when it should only have one!

This is because the burger explosion still surging around Glasgow, with its white noise of slow-cooked pulled pork, wings & ribs, has left behind a gluttonous, wonderfully basted aftermath of top quality burger joints so imposing that it's hard to walk fifty yards here without bumping into one.

The Meat Bar, Ad Lib, Lebowski's, Inn Deep, Cocktail & Burger, Burger Meats Bun, Gourmet Burger Kitchen, Hard Rock & Glasgow's voted best burger at Nice n Sleazy...the list seems endless. And then there's even a few Five Guys now added into the mix!

For me though, topping the lot are Ketchup (for me the southside one at Waverley Tearoom beats its sister in the west end) and its dazzling choice of toppings & burgers, Buddy's with its fiery wings & deep-rooted American BBQ attitude, and Bread Meats Bread's which just screams total innovation.

I don't have the space here to wax lyrical about my love for these places. And hey, Glasgow's now so full of burger joints it's being questioned whether enough's enough, whether we've reached a saturation point. My simple answer is that if you don't like burgers, don't eat them, and if you do, you'll never go hungry here!

contact
See websites for info.

social
buddys.co.uk/
breadmeatsbread.co.uk/
ketchupsouth.co.uk/

when
See websites for info.

where
See websites for info.

top-ten-glasgow-guide.com
facebook.com/toptenglasgowguide
twitter.com/toptenglasgow

WEE GLESGA
A POCKET GUIDE TO GLASGOW

cail bruich

lowdown

I've never been a huge fan of French restaurants in Scotland, but this one makes my top ten without a shadow of doubt. It may be because this is mainly Scots cuisine only influenced by French techniques, or maybe just because as a matter of fact I've never come out of this place thinking anything other than that I'm totally satisfied by what I've just eaten.

Some of the delicious meals I can recommend here are the line caught wild sea bass with cockles, dreamy caramelised cauliflower, grapes & capers; St. Bride's farm chicken with charred leeks & smoked potato; and Loch Duart smoked salmon with heritage beetroot, apple & horseradish.

I don't know why, but the impression I always get from the menu is that the chef has gone out and captured a veritable forest, field & farm of wild food (too many f's?), loved it until it's tame and then, like Michael Caine in Miss Congeniality, finessed it until there's nowt left but purely crafted class. Yeah I know, nonsense, but I can't help how I feel!

I'm not surprised though at the excitement Cail Bruich generates amongst national as well as local food critics; I can speak only for me anyway, and in my mind, dining here combines the best of two countries, one of which is known for its fine dining, and the other which, because of restaurants like this, should be!

contact
Tel: +44 141 334 6265
Email: info@cailbruich.co.uk

social
cailbruich.co.uk/
facebook.com/cailbruich
twitter.com/cailbruich

when
Noon-2.30pm Mon-Sat
5.30pm-9.30pm Mon-Sat
12.30pm-3.30pm Sun
5.300pm-8.00pm Sun

where
725 Great Western Road
Glasgow
G12 8QX

WEE GLESCA
•-•-•
A POCKET GUIDE TO GLASGOW
•-•-•

butchershop bar & grill

lowdown

Although I rave until I drool about the Kobe steak at Grill on the Corner, this place is the only other Glasgow steakhouse I think worthy of proper attention.

Nestled perfectly across from Kelvingrove Art Gallery & Museum and only a walk away from the bustling west end, Finnieston & Hydro, if I'm heading there for a gig or night out I'll usually opt for a grass-fed, 35-day hung & dried black angus t-bone right here.

Absolutely love the butcher's continental charcuterie, which despite it being billed as a starter for two, I've been known to tuck into myself!

It's the atmosphere though that makes me return to this joint time and time again, as I've spent a fair amount of time in NYC and feel in the Butchershop that I'm a stone's throw from Greenwich Village.

If you can make it, I'd definitely head here on a Sunday. The Tafelspitz & roast trimmings is nothing short of jaw-dropping.

As with GOTC though, it's not all about steak here, and the rest of the menu will not disappoint, particularly the Ayrshire pork chop which my wife can't get enough of!

contact
Tel: +44 141 339 2999
Email:
info@butchershopglasgow.com

social
butchershopglasgow.com/
facebook.com/butchershopgl asgow
twitter.com/butchershopgla

when
Noon-11.30pm Sun-Thu
Noon-1am Fri & Sat

where
1055 Sauchiehall Street
Glasgow
G3 7UD

118

top-ten-glasgow-guide.com
facebook.com/toptenglasgowguide
twitter.com/toptenglasgow

WEE GLESGA
A POCKET GUIDE TO GLASGOW

sapporo teppanyaki

lowdown

If you've never had the chance to experience the fun of teppanyaki entertainment, here's the best place in Glasgow to give it a go. Like Khublai Khan's it provides an outstanding talking point which is great for first dates & groups.

Basically you grab a cocktail, choose from the mouth-watering Japanese menus (Shojin Ryori, Shogun, Banzai, Geisha, Samurai, Emperor or sushi variations) grab a starter like the wonderful chicken gyoza and then watch in total bedazzlement as the chef...be it Mr. Big or Superman...in front of you chops and cooks ingredients like a madman, never mind that he'll have done this hundreds of times before with as much enthusiasm, before shouting 'one, two, open your mouth' and firing darts of sautéed potatoes & veg at you all to catch expertly in your mouth (or in my case, in my hair or eyes).

It truly is one of the most fun ways to eat out in the City, and gets rave reviews each and every week. You'll come out of there dizzy from all the sudden flames, flying food, joyful cheers and the mastery of an ancient art that you'll think about with tired fondness as you slowly chop your carrots with a blunt knife at home!

contact

Tel: +44 141 290 0033
Email: info@sapporo.co.uk

social

sapporo.co.uk/restaurant-glasgow/
facebook.com/SapporoTeppanyakiRestaurants
twitter.com/Sapporo_Tepp

when

Noon-11.pm Mon-Sat
Noon-10.30om Sun

where

2-6 Ingram Street
Glasgow
G1 1HA

top-ten-glasgow-guide.com
facebook.com/toptenglasgowguide
twitter.com/toptenglasgow

WEE GLESGA
A POCKET GUIDE TO GLASGOW

street food

lowdown

In the last few years Glasgow's woken up from her deep-fried, greasily calorific nightmare, and embraced the street food revolution with a love known only to out-patients hurtling from a horrifying prognosis!

As a result, these days you'll find less folks eating bags of chips and more meandering around street markets, trucks, warehouses, stalls and pop-ups run by innovative, driven ninjas of the food industry determined to reveal something new and unique, using global flavours at a price welcome to the Glasgow masses still recovering from recession.

Look out particularly for the pioneering Street Food Cartel, including Scoop's amazing Bullet kitchen from the genius behind Ox & Finch, Fire in Babylon's West Indian Rum Shack, pad BKK's vibrant Thai philosophy, the mouth watering pulled pork of Smoak, and the legendary Babu Bombay Street Kitchen which now has a shop so no longer has to prowl the streets.

We're also lucky here to have celebrations of street food in the Street Feastival by offKILTR every year, which has featured the outstanding Harajuku Kitchen, and the Glad Cafe's wonderful Southside Street Food Showdown.

So visitors to Glasgow, whatever you do please don't think you're being authentic by picking your way through a sausage supper. Although I do love the odd one now and again, you'll get a far richer experience of Glasgow's love of food by walking past the chippy & exploring the streets beyond.

social

streetfoodcartel.com
kiltr.com
babu-kitchen.com
thegladcafe.co.uk

top-ten-glasgow-guide.com
facebook.com/toptenglasgowguide
twitter.com/toptenglasgow

WEE GLESCA
A POCKET GUIDE TO GLASGOW

social bite

lowdown

The word on the street has always been that Glasgow's a caring city. "People Make Glasgow" is the glossy slogan for tourists, but break that down and it won't take long before you appreciate the Glaswegian psyche and its tendency to give a monkeys about causes that desperately need attention.

Down the years we've stood in unison for Nelson Mandela, for Ferguson, Charlie Hebdo, Gaza, the Clutha, the Queen Street tragedy in 2014, and countless more causes for charity, inequality & poverty.

Now, in a little sandwich shop called Social Bite, we stand for the homeless & poverty-stricken in our city, the poor in Bangladesh, and the struggling communities in Malawi & Zambia.

With a delicious, well-priced menu created by Michelin Star chef Mike Mathieson, 100% of the profits are donated to these good causes. Every single penny. 1 in 4 of the staff there were formerly homeless, and you can even buy the homeless food & drink via their amazing suspended coffee & food initiative.

So please support what's a truly social business, and give a little back to the community. You really *can* change lives with a sandwich!

contact
Tel: +44 131 220 8206
Email: info@social-bite.co.uk

social
social-bite.co.uk
facebook.com/socialbitebusiness
twitter.com/SocialBite_

when
7am-3pm Mon-Fri

where
103 St. Vincent Street
Glasgow, G2 5EA
& 5 Bothwell Street
Glasgow, G2 6NL

top-ten-glasgow-guide.com
facebook.com/toptenglasgowguide
twitter.com/toptenglasgow

WEE GLESCA
--•--
A POCKET GUIDE TO GLASGOW
--•--

bars

top-ten-glasgow-guide.com
facebook.com/toptenglasgowguide
twitter.com/toptenglasgow

WEE GLESCA

A POCKET GUIDE TO GLASGOW

the glad café

lowdown

The Glad is known in these here parts as the beating heart of the Southside music & arts community. Having previously been involved in setting up local gigs & arts events, in 2012 it got a Social Investment Scotland grant & opened up its own gaff.

Not only is it a swell bar to hang out in, but it's also the community interest hub for the likes of the Southside Fringe, the Glasgow Pop!South Weekender, the fascinating Glad Rag Mag, Glad Academy, Southside Street Food Showdown, Southside Film Festival, the not-for-profit Glad Rags Thrift store and the Glad Foundation affordable music project for local kids.

During the day here you can sip some glorious Dear Green Coffee with delights from the Wild Flours and Big Bear Bakeries, and on any given night you can enjoy live music, speakers, film nights & comedy shows, and as well as a fine menu created by a top local chef. I recommend the Williams beer but more recently West beer's also been served here which I can never turn a blind drunk eye to!

The oomf thrown into this place makes it way more than just some bar, and spending some time here always makes me feel that I'm at the centre of something. Never had a bad night of fun here either, so if you'll be in the Southside, definitely make a point of swinging by.

contact
Tel: +44 141 636 6119
Email: info@thegladcafe.co.uk

social
thegladcafe.co.uk
facebook.com/thegladcafe
twitter.com/thegladcafe

when
9am-11pm Mon-Fri
10am-11pm Sat-Sun

where
1006a Pollokshaws Road
Glasgow
G41 2HG

brewdog

lowdown

You'll likely have heard about BrewDog. It has about 3,000 pubs in the UK (OK, slight exaggeration) and you won't go far in Glasgow now without seeing their bottle-busting ales collection behind whatever bar you're in.

Absolutely LOVE this place. If you're eating here, ask the barkeep for a Killa Morchilla. Nuff said! Drinks-wise, the stunningly myriad selection changes constantly with guest ales rotating as well, so just go there and try a few to sample. My personal favourites here are the original Punk IPA, Jack Hammer and Brixton Porter. If you're not sure what to go for, ask for a little taster board and the staff'll be happy to oblige.

The BrewDog CollabFest is held here as well as in the other BrewDogs around the UK, billed as the biggest collaborative beer festival on the planet, and you'll be able to taste new beers aplenty alongside the usual array of craft-mastery.

There's always a number of free gigs and events in this place as well, so all in you'll have a great time before spilling out into the West End clubs.

Make sure you follow the social media feeds near the time you'll be going, as they're great at keeping you up to date with what's on tap and bottled at that time. I've heard a few complaints recently about BrewDog's blatant commercialisation and in-your-face branding you really can't miss in Glasgow, but what can I say, I'm sold!

contact
Tel: +44 141 334 7175
Email: glasgowbar@brewdog.com

social
brewdog.com/bars/glasgow
facebook.com/brewdogbarglasgow
twitter.com/brewdogglasgow

when
Noon-Midnight Mon-Sat
12.30pm-Midnight Sun

where
1397 Argyle Street
Glasgow
G3 8AN

WEE GLESGA

A POCKET GUIDE TO GLASGOW

west brewery

lowdown

It's not exactly in the best location in town (get a taxi to & from), but if you love Bavarian craft beers and want to experience the brewery in action, sip the beer in the very building it was created rather than in another bar that's just had them delivered, head WEST!

West's nestled snugly inside the spectacular Templeton building (its design inspired by the Palazzo Ducale in Venice) which is pretty famous in Glasgow folklore having housed the world's largest carpet manufacturer that, amongst other things, created carpets for the Titanic & Mrs. Abraham Lincoln.

This historical spirit of ingenuity has been continued with the brewery here. It's the only UK brewery to produce all its lagers & wheat beers in accordance with the Reinheitsgebot, the German Purity Law of 1516 allowing only malted barley, hops, yeast & water to be used, merging centuries of traditional, chemical and additive free practice with state-of-the-art equipment.

Head along to one of their excellent brewery tours there, sample the jovial atmosphere with mouthfuls of Nürnberger Bratwürstl, Jäger Schnitzel & Bavarian Cheese Spätzle washed down nicely with some Munich Red, St. Mungo and Hefeweizen, and I guarantee you'll end the night toasting the Fatherland & developing a penchant for lederhosen!

contact

Tel: +44 141 550 0135
Email: info@westbeer.com

social

westbeer.com
facebook.com/west.beer
twitter.com/Westbeer

when

11am-11pm Sun-Thu
11am-Midnight Fri-Sat

where

Templeton Building
Glasgow Green
Glasgow, G40 1AW

125

top-ten-glasgow-guide.com
facebook.com/toptenglasgowguide
twitter.com/toptenglasgow

WEE GLESGA
A POCKET GUIDE TO GLASGOW

stereo & the old hairdresser's

lowdown

These two vegany, hipstery alternative sisters down the lane (does that sound seedy?) will introduce you to an altogether effortlessly cool side of the City otherwise usually attributed exclusively for the West End.

Barely decorated they're both chilled-out in the day and pretty boisterous at night, with a menu inspired enough to entice folks like me wot ain't vegan, cutting-edge DJs on the decks and arts events in abundance.

The stripped-down decor of Stereo in particular belies the fact that it's housed in one of the most overlooked but sensational buildings of Charles Rennie Mackintosh (see the CRM section earlier) in which the Daily Record newspaper used to operate during WWII.

If you have a night out with one of these two sisters you'll likely be torn love lost between them, as they'll enchant you and leave you with the feeling that your life's just too plain busy & full of things, that you should really go and chill out for a bit and realise it's all ok.

Err, maybe you've been drinking too much here Scott, you might say.

You're probably right there, but either way I'd give them both a try as, aside from anything else, you won't find many places like them elsewhere in town.

contact
Tel: +44 141 222 2254
Email: monostereo@live.co.uk
& theoldhair@gmail.com

social
stereocafebar.com
twitter.com/stereoglasgow
theoldhairdressers.com
twitter.com/OldHairdressers

when
Noon-1am Mon-Wed
Noon-3am Thu-Sun
Old Hairdresser's times vary

where
22-28 & 27 Renfield Lane
Glasgow
G2 6PH

top-ten-glasgow-guide.com
facebook.com/toptenglasgowguide
twitter.com/toptenglasgow

WEE GLESGA
A POCKET GUIDE TO GLASGOW

hillhead bookclub

lowdown

I remember this place as the Salon and then Gong, which really shows my age now so let's move on.

Since HHBC opened some years back I've found as time's gone on that in the West End it's been one of my top choices to start the night before heading to the club at Òran Mór, or to Boho down the road.

"A venue where left and right handers can exist in harmony without fear of persecution."

Don't know why but it's always reminded me of Tom Hanks' place in the movie Big, pretty massive (it used to be a picturehouse) with elaborate cornicing on the high walls, Chesterfields & stag's head but also sprinkled here and there with a caged-off table tennis court & retro gaming machines). Makes for a different atmosphere you might normally expect from a Glasgow pub but hey, I enjoy it!

It has a bit of a cult following, particularly amongst local uni students given the BYOB nights & the quirky events during the week including bingo and vintage fairs, but it's also very welcoming and you'll find it pretty laid-back & comfy to spend some time in.

Jam-jar & teapot cocktails, BrewDog & West beer, fantastic menu that never costs more than a tenner, eclectic mixture of tunes in the background that never drowns out conversation. I just love coming here!

contact
Tel: +44 141 576 1700
Email:
hillheadbookclub.com/contact

social
hillheadbookclub.com
facebook.com/hillheadbookclub
twitter.com/hhbookclub

when
11am-Midnight Mon-Fri
10am-Midnight Sat-Sun

where
17 Vinicombe Street
Glasgow
G12 8SJ

drygate

lowdown

Slap bang in the guts of the oldest area of Glasgow, sitting bravely next to the haunting Necropolis, stands Drygate (which means "Priest's Path" apparently), which at first glance looks to me like some kind of futuristic, industrial prison camp (Crystal Maze, anyone?), but which opens up into one of the snazziest drinking joints in town.

Find a stool next to the floor to ceiling window through to the brewery on site, and sip Bearface lager, Outaspace Apple Ale and Gladeye IPA as they're each created lovingly in front of your eyes.

As with most of the best Glasgow bars, the owners here make an effort. Not only do they brew their own delicious ales and serve up some pretty decent grub at the Vintage & Brewhouse kitchens, but they also invite you to try brewing yourself with the wonderful Studio Kit (great gift for enthusiasts as well as amateurs), lay out for you a regular & free Urban Market, and get you laughing at the Gilded Balloon comedy nights that never disappoint.

There's always something interesting going on here so it's well worth heading off the beaten track for a bit. Any bar can sell beer, but in Glasgow it's crafty, innovative places like this that really make the difference between a night out and a night out you'll want to experience over and over again.

As their tagline suggests, "from the everyday to the exceptional".

contact
Tel: +44 141 212 8815
Email: info@drygate.com

social
drygate.com
facebook.com/drygatebrewingco
twitter.com/drygate

when
11am-Midnight Mon-Sun

where
85 Drygate
Glasgow
G4 0UT

---

top-ten-glasgow-guide.com
facebook.com/toptenglasgowguide
twitter.com/toptenglasgow

WEE GLESGA

A POCKET GUIDE TO GLASGOW

arta

lowdown

This has been my absolute favourite space in Merchant City since it opened.

Think opulence, marble statues, fine cocktails, vibrant vines, Mediterranean baroque hacienda courtyard bar, sprinklings of rose petals to announce the opening of the club downstairs, mesmerising candles.

Sound like a bar to you? Yeah I thought so.

You can spend a whole night in here. Dine in the cavernous restaurant with stunning platters, tapas & continental delicacies, relax in the courtyard with cocktails, then head to one of the clubs downstairs where, depending on the night you go you could find yourself salsa dancing or just making shapes & bustin moves to some fine bands & DJs until the wee hours.

It's a great place for private functions and dining as well, and always provides a central hub to explore the Merchant City Festival every year.

Arta, and the rich grandiosity of the Corinthian just along the road, are for me the two top places to have a classier night out in town. And surprisingly you won't need to break the bank as much as you'd think to spend some time there!

contact
Tel: +44 845 166 6018
Email: arta.co.uk/contact

social
arta.co.uk
facebook.com/artaglasgow
twitter.com/artaglasgow

when
5pm-Midnight Thu
5pm-3am Fri-Sat
Private bookings other days

where
62 Albion Street
Glasgow
G1 1PA

WEE GLESGA
A POCKET GUIDE TO GLASGOW

sloans

lowdown

Glasgow's oldest bar & restaurant, Sloans has been setting out stools for Glasgow punters since 1797.

Folded into the cobbled Argyll Arcade and often hidden from view by the funky Sloans Market (see the shopping section), you'd be forgiven for missing the place.

Don't though, because in the midst of all these craft beer pubs, foreign recreations & trendy bars swirling all around it, Sloans sits at peace as it's done for centuries, smiling to itself maybe, as it raises an eyebrow to all that effort.

Sloans, you see, is pretty much Scotland in a pub. There's other brilliant bars in the City where you'll get a similar feel, of course, but to my mind it's in Sloans more than anywhere else you'll capture what it must've been like generations ago for punters sitting exactly where you are now, sipping Scotland's finest amongst friends.

This feeling's hammered home with the regular ceilidhs in the grand ballroom upstairs, but it's not all about experiencing history here, as their EatFilm meal & a movie events, SMAC nights and comedy gigs will drag you back into this century for a while.

Sloans is a genuine Glasgow institution, so pop in & see why we love it so much that it's still going from strength to strength.

contact

Tel: +44 141 221 8886
Email: info@sloansglasgow.com

social

sloansglasgow.com
facebook.com/sloans1797
twitter.com/sloansglasgow

when

11.30am-Midnight Mon-Thu
11.30am-1am Fri
11am-1am Sat
11am-Midnight Sun

where

62 Argyll Arcade
108 Argyle Street
Glasgow, G2 8BG

top-ten-glasgow-guide.com
facebook.com/toptenglasgowguide
twitter.com/toptenglasgow

WEE GLESGA
A POCKET GUIDE TO GLASGOW

dram!

lowdown

So if you're interested in all things Scottish you'll know that "a wee dram" means a glass of whisky.

In this outstanding watering hole on Woodlands Road you'll find an extensive selection of over 70 malts & blends to keep you going into the wee hours. It also serves Heverlee which is one of my favourite pints, as well as a good range of other beers & wines.

Despite the aged tag normally associated with lovers of whisky, however, Dram! is firmly a place for a more studenty, after-work type crowd, so if a place like this continues to do well then there's hope that Scotland's love of the water of life hasn't abated in the slightest.

They introduced a new smokehouse menu here recently and, to steal from a certain Colonel, it really is finger lickin' good!

There's comedy nights, folk music and quizzes to liven up the place, the tunes are a nice blend of new and old, and the general atmosphere is always pleasant, laid-back and welcoming.

You can even watch some live sports here, a great sign that the owners don't think they're above that kind of thing as do, unfortunately, other snooty joints around town.

I should also say that the staff here are amongst the friendliest I've come across in the City, so props to them for making the effort.

contact
Tel: +44 141 332 1622
Email: dram@maclay.co.uk

social
dramglasgow.co.uk
facebook.com/dramglasgow
twitter.com/Dram_Glasgow

when
Noon-Midnight Mon-Thu
Noon-1am Fri
11am-1am Sat
11am-Midnight Sun

where
232-246 Woodlands Road
Glasgow
G3 6ND

top-ten-glasgow-guide.com
facebook.com/toptenglasgowguide
twitter.com/toptenglasgow

WEE GLESGA
A POCKET GUIDE TO GLASGOW

the pot still

lowdown

So why does a place that sells pie & beans on its menu get into my top 10?

OK I'll give it a go then. One of the premier whisky bars in the world. 566 whiskies from all over the place for sale on an absolutely mesmerising gantry. Fascinating mix every day of regulars, tourists & celebrities, young novices as welcome as old hats. A rich history in spirits distilled in the 19th century.

It's still amazing to me that despite its global reputation the Pot's hardly known to many Glaswegians, and I suspect that's more to do with how it looks from the outside. In the midst of hundreds of shiny, snazzy, trendy bars in the City Centre, the Pot's outward appearance is that of what's known here as an old man's pub. For me, if that really is the reason, then good on it, because I don't think I've been in it when it's not been packed full so I couldn't imagine what it'd be like if even more locals caught onto just how perfect it is.

So if you're in the area, make sure you pop in, let the friendly, knowledgeable staff direct you to a few wee drams to suit your taste, and join the League of Nations sitting next to you to chat about why this place must live on forever!

contact
Tel: +44 141 333 0980
Email: info@thepotstill.co.uk

social
thepotstill.co.uk
facebook.com/ThePotStillGlasgow
twitter.com/potstillglasgow

when
11am-Midnight Mon-Sat
12.30pm-Midnight Sun

where
154 Hope Street
Glasgow
G2 2TH

top-ten-glasgow-guide.com
facebook.com/toptenglasgowguide
twitter.com/toptenglasgow

WEE GLESCA
A POCKET GUIDE TO GLASGOW

thanks again for reading wee glesca

a pocket guide to glasgow
by
scott c. docherty

early 2015 edition

pick up the kindle edition on amazon

Remember, it became the number 1 best selling Glasgow travel guide *because of people like you*, who trusted me enough to spend your hard-earned money on this. I'd love to hear what you think of my little guide, so please remember to leave a wee comment on Amazon or send me some feedback directly.

You can also reach me on Twitter (toptenglasgow) or Facebook (/toptenglasgowguide).

Yours aye,
Scott

top-ten-glasgow-guide.com
facebook.com/toptenglasgowguide
twitter.com/toptenglasgow

WEE GLESCA

A POCKET GUIDE TO GLASGOW

Printed in Poland
by Amazon Fulfillment
Poland Sp. z o.o., Wrocław